CANTABRIA

Travel Guide

Discovery

Your all-in-one handbook for discovering hidden gems, top attractions, relaxation hotspots, culinary delights, and up-to-date tips on the city.

By

Christopher Morrell

N-634a
A-8
Sarón
N-629
Viérnoles
A-67
Pozalagua Cuevas
Ramales de
la Victoria
N-611
N-623
Carranza
Alceda
CANTABRIA
Vega de Pas
Molledo
N-629
N-611
Espinosa De
Los Monteros
Bercedo
N-611
Arija
Torme
Soncillo
Puentedey
Villarcayo
Medina
de Pomar
N-232
A-67
Villalaín

Venture into the heart of Cantabria, where ancient mountains guard timeless secrets and the sea whispers tales of old— are you ready to uncover the mysteries hidden in this northern paradise?

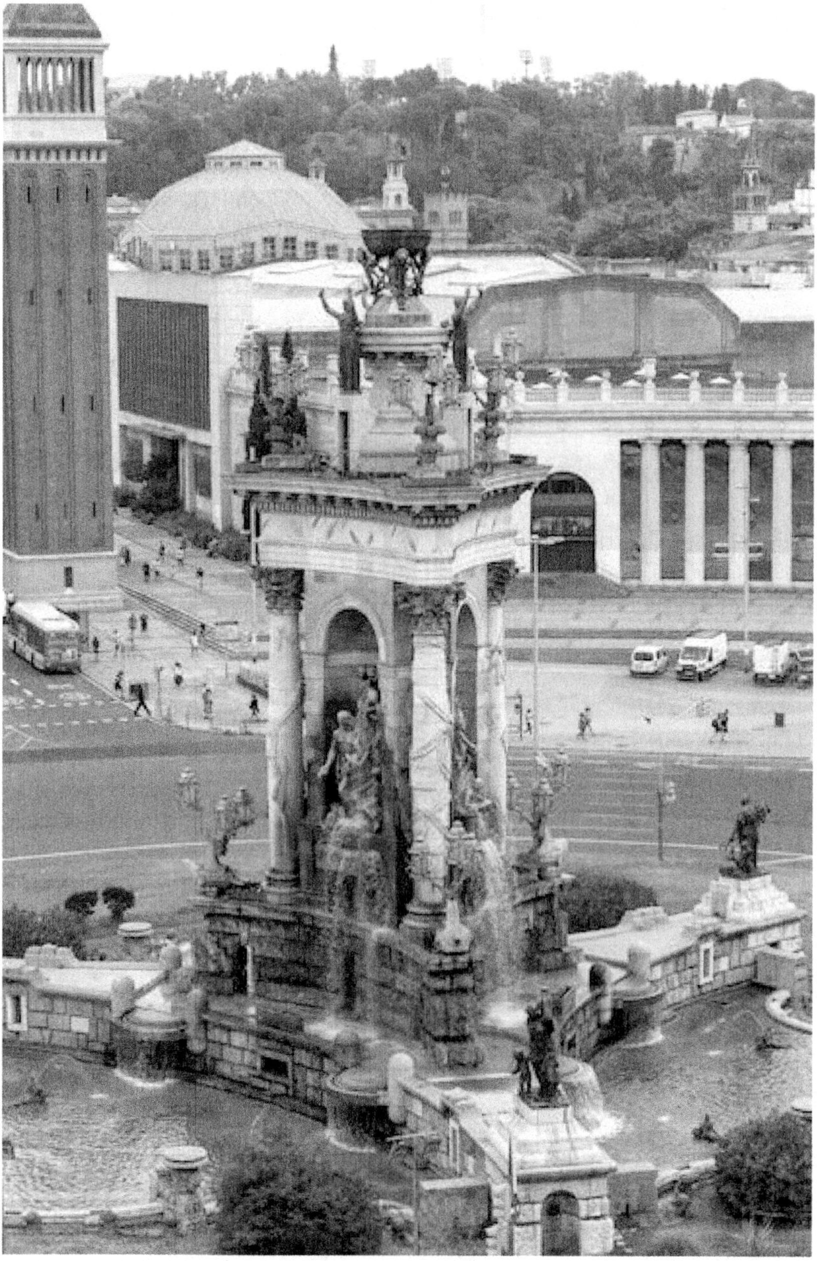

COPYRIGHT NOTICE

This publication is copyright protected. This is only for personal use. No part of this publication may be, including but not limited to, reproduced, in any form or medium, stored in a data retrieval system or transmitted by or through any means, without prior written permission from the Author / Publisher.

Legal action will be pursued if this is breached.

DISCLAIMER

Please note that the information contained within this document is for educational purposes only. The information contained herein has been obtained from sources believed to be reliable at the time of publication. The opinions expressed herein are subject to change without notice.

Readers acknowledge that the Author / Publisher is not engaging in rendering legal, financial or professional advice. The Publisher / Author disclaims all warranties as to the accuracy, completeness, or adequacy of such information.

The Publisher assumes no liability for errors, omissions, or inadequacies in the information contained herein or from the interpretations thereof. The publisher / Author specifically disclaims any liability from the use or application of the information contained herein or from the interpretations thereof.

TABLE OF CONTENT

Introduction 13
   Welcome to Cantabria 13
   Why Visit Cantabria? 14
   How to Use This Guide 15
   A Brief History of Cantabria 16
   Essential Travel Information 17

Chapter 1 19
Getting There and Around 19
   How to Get to Cantabria 19
   Transportation Options in the Region 21
   Renting a Car: Tips and Advice 23
   Public Transport: Buses and Trains 25
   Biking and Walking: Exploring on Foot 26

Chapter 2 30
Top Attractions 30
   Discover Cantabria's Hidden Gems 30
   Must-See Historical Sites 31
   Stunning Parks and Gardens 34
   Unique Museums and Galleries 36
   Iconic Landmarks and Monuments 38

Chapter 3 44
Beaches of Cantabria 44

Why Cantabria's Beaches Are Unique 44
Secluded Paradises for Tranquility Seekers 45
Family-Friendly Beaches 46
Relaxing Coastal Retreats 49
How to Make the Most of Your Beach Visits 50
Beach Safety Tips 52

Chapter 4 55
Outdoor Activities 55
Hiking: Trails for All Levels 55
Water Sports: Kayaking, Surfing, and More 57
Cycling: Routes for Enthusiasts 59
Bird Watching: Discover Rare Species 61
Golf Courses: Best Places to Tee Off 63

Chapter 5 69
Cultural Experiences 69
Traditional Music and Dance 69
Local Festivals: Celebrate with the Cantabrians 71
Art and Craft: Dive into the Culture 73
Handicrafts and Souvenirs: What to Buy and Where 74

Chapter 6 78
Food and Drink 78
Traditional Cantabrian Cuisine 78
Must-Try Dishes and Drinks 80
Top Restaurants and Cafes 82

Farmers' Markets: Fresh and Local....................85
Cooking Classes: Learn to Cook Cantabrian Style.. 86

Chapter 7 91
Itineraries and Sample Plans 91
Weekend Getaway.. 91
Cultural Immersion... 97
Outdoor Adventure..102
Family-Friendly Trip......................................105
Budget Travel...109

Chapter 8 114
Accommodation... 114
Overview of Accommodation Options...............114
Luxury Resorts... 115
Budget-Friendly Hotels..................................116
Boutique Guesthouses...................................117
Unique Stays..118
Top Recommended Hotels and Resorts............120
Choosing the Right Accommodation for You... 122
Booking Tips and Tricks.................................123

Chapter 9 127
Practical Tips and Advice................................... 127
What to Pack for Cantabria............................. 127
Health and Safety Tips.................................. 129
Money Matters: Currency and Budgeting.......... 131

    Etiquette and Local Customs 133
    Do's and Don'ts in Cantabria 135

Chapter 10 139
Enhancing Your Experience 139
    Guided Tours: Why and How to Choose One 139
    Best Times to Visit: Seasonal Highlights 141
    Photography Tips: Capturing the Beauty of
    Cantabria 143
    Day Trips to Nearby Attractions 145
    How to Make Friends with Locals 146

Chapter 11 150
Family Travel Tips 150
    Activities for Kids 150
    Family-Friendly Restaurants 153
    Safety Tips for Families 157
    Stay in Family-Friendly Accommodations 159

Chapter 12 162
Solo Travel 162
    Why Cantabria is Perfect for Solo Travelers ... 162
    Safety Tips for Solo Travelers 163
    Best Activities for Solo Travelers 165

Chapter 13 173
Romantic Getaways 173
    Top Romantic Spots 173

Romantic Activities for Couples 176
Best Restaurants for a Romantic Dinner 178

Chapter 14 .... **183**
Nightlife in Cantabria **183**
   Best Bars and Clubs 183
   Live Music Venues 185
   Nighttime Activities 187

Chapter 15 .... **191**
Shopping in Cantabria **191**
   Best Markets and Shopping Areas 191
   What to Buy: Local Souvenirs and Products 195
   Shopping Tips 197

Chapter 16 .... **201**
Wellness and Relaxation **201**
   Top Spas and Wellness Centers 201
   Yoga and Meditation Retreats 204
   Relaxation Tips 207

Chapter 17 .... **211**
Historical Sites **211**
   Important Historical Landmarks 211
   Stories Behind the Sites 214
   Visiting Tips 218

Chapter 18 .... **221**

Festivals and Events 221
   Major Annual Events 221
   Local Celebrations and Traditions 224
   Planning Your Visit Around Events 227

Appendix 234
Enhance Your Cantabria Experience 234
Map of Cantabria 235
Map of Things to do in Cantabria 236
Glossary: Local Terms 237
Applications and Useful Resources 237
Addresses and Locations of Popular
Accommodations 238
Addresses and Locations of Popular Restaurants
and Cafes 240
Addresses and Locations of Top Attractions 241
Photo Attribution 244

Introduction

Greetings, adventurous souls! If you've picked up this guide, you're likely drawn to the allure of Cantabria, a lesser-known jewel in the crown of Northern Spain. As someone who has traversed its highland trails, relished its rich history, and enjoyed its vibrant local life, I can affirm that Cantabria offers more than just scenic views—it presents an experience that resonates deep within. This guide is more than a collection of maps and tips; it is your gateway to uncovering the soul of Cantabria. Let's set forth on a journey to uncover the myriad charms of this captivating region.

Welcome to Cantabria

Welcome to the heart of northern Spain—Cantabria! Sandwiched between the dramatic peaks of the Cantabrian Mountains and the wild Atlantic coast, this region is a mosaic of breathtaking landscapes, historical depth, and bustling towns. Cantabria is a haven for those who seek the tranquility of nature and the pulse of city life in equal measure. Every landscape, from the lively streets of Santander to the peaceful fishing villages dotting the coastline, has a story waiting to be told. In Cantabria, the past is not a distant echo but a vivid presence that enhances every experience.

Why Visit Cantabria?

What makes Cantabria a must-visit destination on your travel list? Here are ten compelling reasons to explore this stunning region:

1. Spectacular Landscapes: From the lush valleys of Saja-Besaya Natural Park to the breathtaking cliffs along the Costa Quebrada, Cantabria is a nature lover's paradise.

2. Stunning Beaches: Discover the pristine and diverse beaches of Cantabria, perfect for surfing, sunbathing, or simply enjoying the natural beauty.

3. Rich Historical Legacy: Delve into the past with a visit to the Altamira Cave, renowned for its prehistoric paintings, and explore ancient medieval towns.

4. Exquisite Cuisine: Sample the local gastronomy, renowned for its fresh seafood, hearty stews, and the famous Cantabrian anchovies.

5. Vibrant Festivals: Experience local culture through festivals like the Festival of Santander, which fills the region with music, dance, and joy.

6. Outdoor Adventures: Whether it's hiking, caving, or kayaking, Cantabria offers a plethora of activities for the adventurous spirit.

7. Architectural Wonders: Tour architectural marvels from Romanesque churches to modernist buildings in the capital, Santander.

8. Charming Villages: Wander through picturesque villages like Comillas, with its cobblestone streets and historic buildings.

9. Artistic Riches: Explore galleries and museums that showcase both traditional and contemporary art across the region.

10. Thermal Spas: Relax in the thermal waters of Puente Viesgo, which have been appreciated since Roman times for their healing properties.

How to Use This Guide

This guide is crafted to be your comprehensive navigator through Cantabria:

1. Detailed Addresses and Locations: Each recommended site comes with precise addresses to guide your GPS navigation.

2. Up-to-Date Pricing Information: Manage your expenses with current pricing on accommodations, attractions, and dining.

3. Real-Time Directions with Google Maps: Seamlessly find your way from one highlight to another using integrated Google Maps links.

A Brief History of Cantabria

Cantabria's history is rich with tales of Roman conquests, medieval feats, and the timeless traditions of the Cantabri tribes. Known for its strategic importance throughout the centuries, Cantabria's historical narrative is as dramatic as its landscapes, offering insight into the region's enduring spirit and cultural resilience.

Essential Travel Information

Before you embark on your journey, here are ten essential travel tips:

1. Ideal Travel Times: Late spring and early autumn are perfect, offering mild weather and fewer crowds.

2. Currency: The Euro (EUR) is widely accepted here.

3. Language Nuances: Spanish is predominant, though English is commonly understood in tourist areas.

4. Transportation Tips: Renting a car is recommended for exploring remote areas; public transport is reliable in urban centers.

5. Safety Measures: Cantabria is very safe, but standard travel precautions apply.

6. Healthcare Access: Comprehensive travel insurance is recommended; healthcare facilities are excellent.

7. Cultural Etiquette: Embrace the laid-back local lifestyle and late dining culture.

8. Packing Essentials: Weather can be variable, so pack layers and waterproof gear.

9. Connectivity: Wi-Fi is widely accessible, but rural areas may have spotty coverage.

10. Regulatory Compliance: Be aware of local laws to ensure a smooth trip.

Are You Ready to Discover Cantabria?

Turn the page and dive deeper into what Cantabria has to offer. This guide is designed to ensure that your journey through Cantabria is not just a visit, but a memorable exploration of a land where history and modernity dance in harmony. Your adventure in Cantabria starts now—embrace it, and it promises to be one of your most unforgettable experiences!

Chapter 1

Getting There and Around

How to Get to Cantabria

If you're reading this, you're probably considering a trip to Cantabria, and let me tell you, you're in for a treat. Nestled on Spain's northern coast, Cantabria is a region of lush landscapes, dramatic coastlines, and charming towns. My first trip to Cantabria was a revelation; the region felt like a hidden gem waiting to be discovered. Getting there is relatively straightforward, whether you're flying, driving, or taking a train.

By Air: The quickest way to reach Cantabria is by flying into Santander Airport (SDR), located just a few kilometers from Santander, the capital of Cantabria. The airport is small but efficient, with connections to major Spanish cities like Madrid and Barcelona, as well as some international destinations. I flew from Madrid, and the flight was just about an hour. Once you land, it's easy to catch a bus or taxi into the city center.

Santander Airport

Address: Carretera del aeropuerto, s/n, 39600 Maliaño, Cantabria

Phone: +34 942 202 100

By Train: If you prefer a scenic route, the train ride from Madrid to Santander is a fantastic option. The Renfe Alvia trains are comfortable and offer stunning views of the Spanish countryside. The journey takes about four hours, making it a relaxing way to travel. I once took this train, and watching the landscape transition from the arid plains of Castilla y León to the green hills of Cantabria was mesmerizing.

Santander Train Station

Address: Plaza de las Estaciones, s/n, 39002 Santander, Cantabria

Phone: +34 912 320 320

By Car: Driving to Cantabria gives you the flexibility to explore at your own pace. The highways are well-maintained, and the drive from Madrid takes about five hours. I rented a car for one of my trips and loved the freedom it gave me to stop at small villages and scenic viewpoints along the way. The A-67 motorway leads directly into Cantabria, making the journey straightforward.

Transportation Options in the Region

Once you're in Cantabria, getting around is easy, thanks to a variety of transportation options. Whether you prefer the independence of driving or the convenience of public transport, Cantabria has you covered.

Car Rental: Renting a car is the best way to explore Cantabria's diverse landscapes. From the coastal cliffs to the mountainous interior, having a car lets you discover hidden gems off the beaten path. On one trip, I rented a car from Europcar in Santander and drove to the Picos de Europa National Park. The drive was spectacular, with winding roads and breathtaking views.

Europcar Santander

Address: Calle Aeropuerto, s/n, 39600 Maliaño, Cantabria

Phone: +34 902 105 030

Buses: Cantabria has a reliable bus network that connects major towns and cities. ALSA is the main operator, and their buses are comfortable and punctual. I used the bus to travel from Santander to Santillana del Mar, a charming medieval village. The journey was smooth, and the bus dropped me off right in the village center.

ALSA Bus Service

Customer Service Phone: +34 902 422 242

Trains: The regional train service in Cantabria is operated by Renfe Feve. These narrow-gauge trains are perfect for scenic journeys along the coast and through the mountains. I took the Feve train from

Santander to the coastal town of Comillas, and it was a delightful experience. The train wound its way through picturesque landscapes, making the journey as enjoyable as the destination.

Renfe Feve

Customer Service Phone: +34 912 320 320

Taxis and Rideshares: Taxis are readily available in urban areas like Santander and Torrelavega. You can hail a taxi on the street, find one at designated stands, or call for a pickup. Ridesharing services like Uber and Cabify are also available, providing convenient options for getting around.

Radiotaxi Santander

Phone: +34 942 333 333

Renting a Car: Tips and Advice

Renting a car in Cantabria is a great way to explore the region's natural beauty and historic sites. Here are some tips based on my experiences:

Book in Advance: Especially during the summer months, it's a good idea to book your car rental in advance. This ensures you get the vehicle you want and can save you money.

Choose the Right Car: The roads in Cantabria can vary from highways to narrow mountain roads. I recommend a compact car for easier maneuverability, especially if you plan to explore rural areas.

Check for Insurance: Make sure your rental includes comprehensive insurance. It's better to be covered for any eventuality. During one trip, a minor scratch could have been a costly affair without insurance.

Understand the Fuel Policy: Some rental companies require you to return the car with a full tank of gas, while others have different policies. Be clear on this to avoid extra charges.

GPS and Maps: While many cars come with GPS, having a paper map as a backup can be helpful. I found myself in areas with poor GPS signal, and my trusty map saved the day.

Parking: Parking in cities like Santander can be challenging, but there are plenty of parking garages. In smaller towns and rural areas, parking is generally easier. Always check parking signs to avoid fines.

Public Transport: Buses and Trains

Public transport in Cantabria is both efficient and affordable, making it a great option for those who prefer not to drive.

Buses: The bus network covers most of the region, connecting cities, towns, and villages. The buses are clean, comfortable, and usually on time. On one of my trips, I used the ALSA bus service to travel from Santander to Potes, the gateway to the Picos de Europa. The bus ride was comfortable and offered stunning views of the countryside.

ALSA Bus Service

Customer Service Phone: +34 902 422 242

Trains: Renfe Feve operates narrow-gauge trains that run through Cantabria's most scenic areas. The trains are slower than buses but offer a unique travel experience. I took the Feve train from Santander to Laredo, a lovely coastal town with a beautiful beach. The train ride was relaxing, with plenty of opportunities to take in the views.

Renfe Feve

Customer Service Phone: +34 912 320 320

Commuter Trains: For shorter trips within the region, the commuter train service is very convenient. These trains are frequent and connect key locations quickly and efficiently. I often used the commuter train to travel between Santander and Torrelavega, a bustling market town.

Biking and Walking: Exploring on Foot

Cantabria is a paradise for those who enjoy biking and walking. The region's diverse landscapes offer endless opportunities for exploration.

Biking: With its rolling hills and coastal paths, Cantabria is perfect for cycling enthusiasts. Many towns have bike rental shops, and the roads are generally bike-friendly. I rented a bike in Santander and rode along the Sardinero beach promenade, which was an exhilarating experience. The sea breeze and the stunning views made it a highlight of my trip.

Santander Cycles

Address: Calle Cádiz, 13, 39002 Santander, Cantabria

Phone: +34 942 222 200

Walking: Whether you're an avid hiker or just enjoy a leisurely stroll, Cantabria has something for everyone. The Camino de Santiago passes through the region, offering well-marked trails with beautiful scenery. One of my favorite walks was along the coastline from Santoña to Laredo. The path took me through cliffs, beaches, and small fishing villages, each turn revealing another breathtaking view.

Camino de Santiago Information

Phone: +34 981 568 846

Urban Walking: Exploring Cantabria's cities and towns on foot is also a joy. Santander, with its elegant boulevards and historic buildings, is perfect for a walking tour. I loved wandering through the Mercado de la Esperanza, the city's central market, where the vibrant stalls and local produce provided a feast for the senses.

Mercado de la Esperanza

Address: Plaza de la Esperanza, s/n, 39002 Santander, Cantabria

Phone: +34 942 200 870

Nature Trails: For a more immersive nature experience, the Saja-Besaya Natural Park offers numerous trails through dense forests and along pristine rivers. I spent a day hiking there, and the tranquility and beauty of the park were unforgettable. The trails are well-maintained and cater to all levels of hikers.

Saja-Besaya Natural Park

Address: Barrio La Molina, s/n, 39409 Los Tojos, Cantabria

Phone: +34 942 049 438

In summary, getting to and around Cantabria is part of the adventure. Whether you choose to drive, take public transport, or explore on foot or by bike, you'll find that the journey is just as enjoyable as the destinations. Each mode of transport offers its own unique perspective of this stunning region. I hope these tips and personal experiences help you navigate and enjoy Cantabria to the fullest. Safe travels and happy exploring!

Chapter 2

Top Attractions

Discover Cantabria's Hidden Gems

Cantabria is a region that captivated me from the moment I arrived. Nestled between the mountains and the sea in northern Spain, it offers a rich tapestry of experiences, from stunning natural landscapes to historical treasures. My journey through Cantabria was filled with delightful surprises and hidden gems that I'm excited to share with you.

One of my favorite discoveries was San Vicente de la Barquera, a charming fishing village with stunning coastal views. The town is famous for its picturesque harbor and the beautiful Puente de la Maza bridge. I spent a wonderful afternoon walking along the waterfront, enjoying the salty sea breeze and watching the fishing boats bobbing in the water. The village also has some fantastic seafood restaurants, where you can enjoy fresh catches of the day. If you're in the area, don't miss El Retiro.

El Retiro

Address: Calle Alta, 10, 39540 San Vicente de la Barquera, Cantabria

Phone: +34 942 71 20 33

Another hidden gem is the Cueva El Soplao, a spectacular cave system renowned for its unique geological formations. The guided tour took us deep into the earth, where we marveled at the stunning stalactites and stalagmites. The cave is also famous for its helictites, which are rare, twisted formations that seem to defy gravity. It's an otherworldly experience that's not to be missed.

Cueva El Soplao

Address: Lugar Barrio Celis, s/n, 39553 Celis, Cantabria

Phone: +34 902 82 02 82

Must-See Historical Sites

Cantabria is steeped in history, and there are several historical sites that offer a glimpse into the region's rich past. One of the most impressive is the Cave of Altamira. Known as the "Sistine Chapel of Prehistoric Art," this cave contains some of the world's finest examples of Paleolithic cave paintings. Although the original cave is closed to the public to preserve the artwork, the nearby museum features a meticulous replica that allows you to experience the awe-inspiring paintings up close.

Cave of Altamira

Address: Calle Marcelino Sanz de Sautuola, s/n, 39330 Santillana del Mar, Cantabria

Phone: +34 942 81 80 05

In the heart of Santillana del Mar, one of Spain's most beautiful villages, you'll find the Collegiate Church of Santillana del Mar. This stunning Romanesque church dates back to the 12th century and is renowned for its beautiful cloister and detailed carvings. I loved wandering through the cobblestone streets of the village, soaking in the medieval atmosphere before stepping into the serene courtyard of the church.

Collegiate Church of Santillana del Mar

Address: Plaza Abad Francisco Navarro, s/n, 39330 Santillana del Mar, Cantabria

Phone: +34 942 81 80 17

Another historical highlight is Comillas, a town known for its modernist architecture. The standout is El Capricho de Gaudí, a whimsical villa designed by the famous architect Antoni Gaudí. The building's intricate designs and vibrant colors are a feast for the eyes, and the guided tour provided fascinating insights into Gaudí's unique vision.

El Capricho de Gaudí

Address: Barrio Sobrellano, s/n, 39520 Comillas, Cantabria

Phone: +34 942 72 03 65

Stunning Parks and Gardens

Cantabria's natural beauty is showcased in its many parks and gardens, which offer tranquil retreats from the hustle and bustle of daily life. One of my favorite spots was the Parque de la Naturaleza de Cabárceno. This sprawling nature park is home to a wide variety of animals living in large, natural enclosures. I spent a whole day exploring the park, watching elephants roam the grassy fields and spotting gorillas in the lush forested areas. The park also features beautiful landscapes, including limestone formations and tranquil lakes.

Parque de la Naturaleza de Cabárceno

Address: 39627 Obregón, Cantabria

Phone: +34 942 56 38 08

In the heart of Santander, the Jardines de Piquío offer stunning views of the coastline and a peaceful place to relax. The gardens are perched on a small promontory, providing panoramic views of the sandy beaches and the sparkling Bay of Biscay. It's a perfect spot for a leisurely stroll or a quiet moment of reflection.

Jardines de Piquío

Address: Av. de la Reina Victoria, 39005 Santander, Cantabria

Phone: +34 942 20 30 00

For a more immersive natural experience, head to the Saja-Besaya Natural Park. This expansive park is a paradise for hikers and nature lovers, with its dense forests, rushing rivers, and abundant wildlife. I embarked on a memorable hike along the Ruta de los Foramontanos, a historic trail that offers breathtaking views of the surrounding mountains and valleys.

Saja-Besaya Natural Park

Address: Barrio La Molina, s/n, 39409 Los Tojos, Cantabria

Phone: +34 942 049 438

Unique Museums and Galleries

Cantabria boasts a rich cultural scene, with museums and galleries that cater to a wide range of interests. One of the most fascinating is the Museum of Prehistory and Archaeology of Cantabria. The museum's extensive collection includes artifacts from the region's prehistoric, Roman, and medieval periods. I was particularly captivated by the display of tools and artwork from the Paleolithic era, which provided a tangible connection to the distant past.

Museum of Prehistory and Archaeology of Cantabria

Address: Calle Bailén, s/n, 39004 Santander, Cantabria

Phone: +34 942 20 72 23

Art enthusiasts should not miss the Centro Botín, a contemporary art center designed by renowned architect Renzo Piano. The building itself is a work of art, with its sleek, modern design and stunning views of the bay. Inside, the galleries feature a rotating selection of contemporary art exhibitions. I was lucky enough to catch an exhibition of works by Spanish artists, which was both thought-provoking and visually stunning.

Centro Botín

Address: Muelle de Albareda, s/n, 39004 Santander, Cantabria

Phone: +34 942 04 20 00

Another unique museum is the Museo Marítimo del Cantábrico. This maritime museum explores the region's rich seafaring history, with exhibits on everything from traditional fishing techniques to modern marine biology. The highlight for me was the aquarium, where I spent hours watching the colorful fish and majestic sea turtles glide through the water.

Museo Marítimo del Cantábrico

Address: San Martín de Bajamar, s/n, 39004 Santander, Cantabria

Phone: +34 942 27 49 62

Iconic Landmarks and Monuments

Cantabria is home to several iconic landmarks and monuments that are a testament to the region's rich history and culture. One of the most impressive is the Palacio de la Magdalena. This grand palace, perched on a hill overlooking the sea, was once the summer residence of the Spanish royal family. Today, it's open to the public, and I spent a delightful afternoon exploring its opulent rooms and beautiful gardens. The panoramic views from the palace grounds are simply breathtaking.

Palacio de la Magdalena

Address: Av. de la Reina Victoria, s/n, 39005 Santander, Cantabria

Phone: +34 942 20 30 84

Another must-see landmark is the Torre del Oro, an ancient watchtower that offers a glimpse into

Cantabria's medieval past. The tower's strategic location provided a vantage point to spot approaching ships, and today it offers visitors stunning views of the surrounding countryside. Climbing to the top of the tower was a bit of a workout, but the view was well worth the effort.

Torre del Oro

Address: Calle de los Azogues, 13, 39300 Torrelavega, Cantabria

Phone: +34 942 80 12 50

In the town of Castro Urdiales, the Iglesia de Santa María de la Asunción is a Gothic masterpiece that dominates the skyline. The church's soaring spires and intricate stained glass windows are a sight to behold. Inside, the atmosphere is serene and contemplative, providing a peaceful retreat from the bustling town.

Iglesia de Santa María de la Asunción

Address: Plaza del Ayuntamiento, s/n, 39700 Castro Urdiales, Cantabria

Phone: +34 942 86 00 97

One of Cantabria's most iconic natural landmarks is the Picos de Europa National Park. This stunning mountain range offers some of the best hiking and outdoor activities in Spain. I embarked on a challenging but rewarding hike to the Fuente Dé cable car, which whisked me up to a breathtaking viewpoint. The panoramic views of the rugged peaks and verdant valleys were unforgettable, and it's an experience I highly recommend.

Picos de Europa National Park

Address: Calle Mayor, 2, 39570 Potes, Cantabria

Phone: +34 942 73 81 07

My Personal Experience in Cantabria

Cantabria left an indelible mark on me, with its rich history, stunning landscapes, and warm hospitality.

One of the highlights of my trip was exploring the Picos de Europa National Park. The sheer beauty of the mountains took my breath away, and the sense of tranquility I felt while hiking through the park was unparalleled. I still remember sitting on a rock, overlooking the valley, and feeling a profound connection to nature.

Another memorable experience was visiting the Cave of Altamira. Standing in front of the replica paintings, I was struck by the realization that I was looking at artwork created by our ancient ancestors tens of thousands of years ago. It was a humbling and awe-inspiring moment that connected me to the deep history of humanity.

The coastal charm of San Vicente de la Barquera also left a lasting impression. The combination of scenic beauty, historical sites, and friendly locals made my visit truly special. I found myself returning to the village's quaint harbor multiple times, each visit revealing new facets of its charm.

In Santander, I enjoyed the vibrant urban life balanced with serene coastal beauty. The city's mix of modern amenities and historical sites provided a well-rounded experience. I spent many afternoons strolling through the Jardines de Piquío, appreciating the peacefulness and the stunning views of the Bay of Biscay.

The culinary delights of Cantabria were another highlight. From savoring fresh seafood in San Vicente de la Barquera to enjoying traditional Cantabrian dishes in small village restaurants, each meal was a journey of discovery. One particularly memorable meal was at El Retiro in San Vicente de la Barquera, where the flavors of the sea were perfectly captured in every dish.

Cantabria is a region that invites exploration and offers rewards at every turn. Whether you're drawn to its rich history, stunning natural beauty, or vibrant culture, there's something here for every traveler. My time in Cantabria was filled with unforgettable experiences and heartfelt connections, making it a destination I'll always hold dear.

I hope this guide inspires you to discover the many treasures of Cantabria and create your own memorable journey. Safe travels and enjoy every moment in this beautiful region of Spain!

Chapter 3

Beaches of Cantabria

Cantabria, Spain, has some of the most beautiful and varied beaches I've ever had the pleasure of visiting. From tranquil coves to expansive sands, Cantabria's coastline offers something for every kind of beachgoer. Here, I'll share my experiences and tips to help you make the most of your beach visits in this stunning region.

Why Cantabria's Beaches Are Unique

Cantabria's beaches are unique because of their diversity and natural beauty. Unlike the more commercialized beaches of Spain, Cantabria's shores often feel untouched and serene. The backdrop of rugged cliffs, rolling green hills, and charming coastal villages adds a special charm to every beach outing. Whether you're looking for solitude, family fun, or an adrenaline rush, Cantabria has a beach for you.

Secluded Paradises for Tranquility Seekers

If you're like me and enjoy escaping the crowds, Cantabria offers several secluded beaches where you can unwind and soak in the natural beauty. One of my favorite spots is Playa de Langre, a hidden gem surrounded by towering cliffs. The beach is divided into two parts, Langre Grande and Langre Pequeño. The walk down to the beach can be a bit steep, but the effort is well worth it. The golden sand and turquoise waters create a perfect setting for relaxation.

Playa de Langre

Location: Langre, Cantabria

Contact: Tourist Information Office, Calle de la Concordia, 3, 39160 Langre. Phone: +34 942 505 064

Another tranquil spot is Playa de Oyambre, located within the Oyambre Natural Park. This beach offers stunning views of the Picos de Europa mountains in the background. The vast stretch of sand means you can always find a quiet spot to lay your towel. It's also a great place for a leisurely walk along the shore, with the sound of the waves providing a soothing soundtrack.

Playa de Oyambre

Location: San Vicente de la Barquera, Cantabria

Contact: Oyambre Natural Park Visitor Center, Barrio de la Barquera, s/n, 39540 San Vicente de la Barquera. Phone: +34 942 846 351

Family-Friendly Beaches

Traveling with family means finding beaches that are safe and have plenty of amenities. Playa de Comillas is one of the best family-friendly beaches in Cantabria. The shallow waters make it perfect for young children to splash around safely, and there are plenty of nearby cafes and restaurants for when you need a break. I spent a delightful afternoon here with my nieces, building sandcastles and enjoying ice cream from one of the local vendors.

Playa de Comillas

Location: Comillas, Cantabria

Contact: Comillas Tourist Office, Plaza del Corro de San Pedro, s/n, 39520 Comillas. Phone: +34 942 724 617

Another great family beach is Playa de Berria in Santoña. This beach is wide and flat, making it ideal for games and picnics. Lifeguards are on duty during the summer months, providing an extra level of safety. The nearby marshes and dunes are also fun to explore, and you might even spot some local wildlife.

Playa de Berria

Location: Santoña, Cantabria

Contact: Santoña Tourist Office, Plaza San Antonio, 3, 39740 Santoña. Phone: +34 942 662 890

Adventurous Beach Escapes

For those seeking adventure, Cantabria's beaches do not disappoint. Playa de Somo is renowned for its excellent surfing conditions. The consistent waves and surf schools make it a perfect spot for both beginners and experienced surfers. I took a beginner's surf lesson here and had an absolute blast. The instructors were friendly and patient, making it a fun and rewarding experience.

Playa de Somo

Location: Somo, Cantabria

Contact: Escuela Cantabra de Surf, Calle Isla de Mouro, 10, 39140 Somo. Phone: +34 942 510 615

If surfing isn't your thing, Playa de los Locos in Suances offers thrilling waves for bodyboarding. The dramatic cliffs and strong currents make this beach more suitable for experienced water enthusiasts. Watching the sunset from the cliffs here is a breathtaking experience that I highly recommend.

Playa de los Locos

Location: Suances, Cantabria

Contact: Suances Tourist Office, Plaza Viares, 1, 39340 Suances. Phone: +34 942 811 811

Relaxing Coastal Retreats

Sometimes, you just need to unwind and let the world drift by. Playa de La Arnía is the perfect place for this. Nestled between striking rock formations, this beach offers a peaceful escape from the hustle and bustle. The views are spectacular, and it's a fantastic spot for photography or simply enjoying a good book. I spent a serene afternoon here, letting the sound of the waves and the stunning scenery wash over me.

Playa de La Arnía

Location: Liencres, Cantabria

Contact: Tourist Information Office, Barrio La Arnía, 16, 39120 Liencres. Phone: +34 942 575 284

Playa de Ris in Noja is another great retreat. This beach is expansive, with plenty of space to find your own private nook. The calm waters are perfect for a gentle swim, and there are several beachfront bars where you can enjoy a refreshing drink. I loved ending my day here with a leisurely stroll along the shoreline, watching the waves roll in.

Playa de Ris

Location: Noja, Cantabria

Contact: Noja Tourist Office, Paseo Marítimo, s/n, 39180 Noja. Phone: +34 942 631 072

How to Make the Most of Your Beach Visits

Making the most of your beach visits in Cantabria involves a bit of planning and a sense of adventure. Here are some tips I've picked up during my travels:

Check the Tides: Many of Cantabria's beaches change dramatically with the tides. Before you head out, check the local tide charts. This can help you avoid disappointment if you're looking for a sandy stretch that might be underwater at high tide.

Pack a Picnic: While there are plenty of cafes and bars, bringing your own picnic allows you to stay longer and enjoy more remote spots. I always pack some local cheese, fresh bread, and a bottle of wine. It's a delightful way to experience the region's culinary delights.

Bring the Right Gear: Depending on your plans, make sure you have the appropriate gear. For a relaxing day, bring a good book, sunscreen, and a comfortable beach chair. If you're planning on water sports, ensure you have your wetsuit, board, and any other necessary equipment.

Explore the Surroundings: Many of Cantabria's beaches are near interesting sites and hiking trails. Combining a beach day with a bit of exploration can make for a more enriching experience. I love hiking the trails around Playa de Oyambre before cooling off in the sea.

Respect the Environment: Cantabria's natural beauty is one of its greatest assets. Always clean up after yourself and respect the local wildlife. Some beaches are part of protected areas, so follow any posted guidelines to help preserve these wonderful places.

Beach Safety Tips

Safety is paramount when enjoying Cantabria's beaches. Here are some essential tips to ensure a safe and fun visit:

Swim in Designated Areas: Many beaches have specific areas designated for swimming. These zones are monitored by lifeguards and are usually the safest spots. Always pay attention to the flags indicating the safety of the water (green for safe, yellow for caution, and red for dangerous).

Be Aware of Currents: Some of Cantabria's beaches, like Playa de los Locos, have strong currents. Always stay within your swimming abilities and avoid swimming alone in unfamiliar waters.

Sun Protection: The sun in Cantabria can be quite strong, especially during the summer months. Always wear sunscreen, a hat, and sunglasses. I also recommend bringing a beach umbrella for some shade during the hottest parts of the day.

Hydration: Staying hydrated is crucial, especially if you're spending the whole day at the beach. Bring plenty of water and drink regularly to avoid dehydration.

First Aid: It's always a good idea to have a basic first aid kit on hand. Cuts and scrapes from rocks or shells can happen, and it's better to be prepared. Many beaches have first aid stations, but having your own supplies can be handy.

Local Advice: When in doubt, ask the locals. Lifeguards, beach vendors, and fellow beachgoers can offer valuable advice and insights. During my visits, I've found that people are always willing to help and share their knowledge about the best spots and safety tips.

Cantabria's beaches are a treasure trove of natural beauty and diverse experiences. From secluded coves to family-friendly sands and adventurous surf spots, there's something for everyone. My time spent exploring these stunning beaches has been filled with unforgettable moments, and I hope this guide helps you create your own amazing memories in Cantabria. Whether you're seeking tranquility, family fun, or thrilling adventures, Cantabria's coastline awaits you with open arms. Enjoy your beach adventures and stay safe!

Chapter 4

Outdoor Activities

Cantabria, Spain, is an outdoor enthusiast's paradise, offering a wide range of activities that cater to all tastes and fitness levels. From its rugged coastlines to its verdant mountains, every corner of this region invites you to explore and reconnect with nature. During my time in Cantabria, I found myself constantly in awe of its natural beauty and the sheer variety of outdoor adventures it offers. Here's a detailed look at some of the best outdoor activities you can enjoy in this stunning part of Spain.

Hiking: Trails for All Levels

Cantabria's hiking trails are as diverse as its landscapes, ranging from gentle coastal walks to challenging mountain treks. One of my favorite hikes was along the Camino del Norte, part of the famous Camino de Santiago. This route offers spectacular views of the Cantabrian Sea and takes you through charming fishing villages and lush green fields.

Address: Camino del Norte, Cantabria, Spain

Phone: +34 942 31 89 64 (Tourist Information Office)

For those seeking a more challenging hike, the Picos de Europa National Park is a must-visit. The park is home to some of the most breathtaking scenery in Spain, with towering peaks, deep gorges, and pristine lakes. I hiked the Ruta del Cares, a stunning trail that follows the Cares River through a narrow gorge. The trail is about 12 kilometers long and offers dramatic views at every turn.

Address: Picos de Europa National Park, Cantabria, Spain

Phone: +34 942 73 84 00 (Park Information Center)

For a gentler hike, the Senda Fluvial del Nansa is perfect. This trail follows the Nansa River and takes you through serene forests and past picturesque villages. It's a great option for families and those looking for a leisurely walk.

Address: Senda Fluvial del Nansa, Cantabria, Spain

Phone: +34 942 84 89 00 (Tourist Information Office)

Water Sports: Kayaking, Surfing, and More

Cantabria's coastline is a haven for water sports enthusiasts. From kayaking to surfing, there's something for everyone. During my stay, I had the chance to try both, and each experience was unforgettable.

Kayaking on the Sella River was a highlight of my trip. The river winds through beautiful countryside and offers a peaceful yet exhilarating way to explore the region. I rented a kayak from a local outfitter and spent a day paddling along the gentle waters, surrounded by stunning scenery.

Address: Sella River, Cantabria, Spain

Phone: +34 942 71 27 28 (Kayak Rentals)

Surfing is another popular activity in Cantabria, thanks to its consistent waves and beautiful beaches. Playa de Somo is one of the best spots for surfing, with waves suitable for both beginners and experienced surfers. I took a surfing lesson at a local surf school, and the instructors were fantastic—patient, knowledgeable, and incredibly friendly.

Address: Playa de Somo, Cantabria, Spain

Phone: +34 942 50 20 60 (Surf School)

For those who prefer a more relaxed water experience, Playa de Oyambre offers a beautiful setting for swimming and sunbathing. The beach is part of the Oyambre Natural Park, and its unspoiled beauty is perfect for a day of relaxation by the sea.

Address: Playa de Oyambre, Cantabria, Spain

Phone: +34 942 74 89 00 (Natural Park Information)

Cycling: Routes for Enthusiasts

Cycling is a fantastic way to explore Cantabria's diverse landscapes. Whether you're a seasoned cyclist or a casual rider, you'll find plenty of routes to suit your level.

One of the most popular cycling routes is the Vía Verde del Pas, a former railway line that has been converted into a scenic cycling path. The route is relatively flat and takes you through beautiful countryside, charming villages, and along the Pas River. I rented a bike in Ontaneda and spent a delightful day cycling this trail, stopping for a picnic by the river and enjoying the peaceful surroundings.

Address: Vía Verde del Pas, Cantabria, Spain

Phone: +34 942 59 81 32 (Bike Rentals)

For more experienced cyclists, the Ruta de los Puertos offers a challenging ride through the mountains. This route includes several steep climbs and offers breathtaking views of the surrounding peaks and valleys. It's a tough ride, but the sense of accomplishment and the stunning vistas make it well worth the effort.

Address: Ruta de los Puertos, Cantabria, Spain

Phone: +34 942 76 00 75 (Tourist Information Office)

Another great option is the Ruta de los Picos, which takes you through the Picos de Europa National Park. This route is known for its spectacular scenery and diverse terrain, making it a favorite among cycling enthusiasts. I joined a guided cycling tour, which was a fantastic way to learn more about the park and its natural wonders while enjoying a challenging ride.

Address: Picos de Europa National Park, Cantabria, Spain

Phone: +34 942 73 84 00 (Park Information Center)

Bird Watching: Discover Rare Species

Cantabria is a paradise for bird watchers, with its varied habitats supporting a wide range of bird species. During my time in the region, I had the chance to visit several top bird-watching spots and was amazed by the diversity of birds I encountered.

One of the best places for bird watching is the Marismas de Santoña, Victoria y Joyel Natural Park. This coastal wetland is home to numerous bird species, including herons, ospreys, and various types of ducks and waders. I joined a guided bird-watching tour, and the knowledgeable guide helped me spot several rare species that I might have otherwise missed.

Address: Marismas de Santoña, Victoria y Joyel Natural Park, Cantabria, Spain

Phone: +34 942 63 11 02 (Park Information)

Another excellent bird-watching location is the Collados del Asón Natural Park. This park's diverse habitats, including forests, meadows, and cliffs, attract a wide variety of birds. I spent a day hiking through the park, binoculars in hand, and was thrilled to spot several birds of prey, including the majestic golden eagle.

Address: Collados del Asón Natural Park, Cantabria, Spain

Phone: +34 942 67 81 50 (Park Information)

For those interested in sea birds, the Cabo de Ajo is a great spot. The rugged cliffs and rocky shores provide excellent nesting sites for a variety of seabirds. I visited in the early morning, and the sight of birds soaring over the waves, with the sun rising in the background, was simply magical.

Address: Cabo de Ajo, Cantabria, Spain

Phone: +34 942 26 11 07 (Tourist Information Office)

Golf Courses: Best Places to Tee Off

Golf enthusiasts will find plenty to love in Cantabria, with several top-notch courses set in beautiful surroundings. Whether you're a seasoned pro or a beginner, you'll find a course that suits your skill level.

Real Golf de Pedreña is one of the most prestigious golf courses in the region. Located on a peninsula overlooking the Bay of Santander, this course offers stunning views and a challenging layout. I had the pleasure of playing a round here, and the combination of the beautiful scenery and the well-maintained course made for an unforgettable experience.

Address: Barrio Pedreña, s/n, 39130 Pedreña, Cantabria, Spain

Phone: +34 942 50 70 25

Another excellent option is the Santa Marina Golf Club, designed by the legendary Spanish golfer Seve

Ballesteros. This course is set in a beautiful valley and offers a challenging but fair test of golf. The club also has excellent facilities, including a driving range and a clubhouse with a great restaurant. I spent a lovely day here, enjoying both the golf and the stunning natural surroundings.

Address: Barrio Escagedo, 39549 San Vicente de la Barquera, Cantabria, Spain

Phone: +34 942 72 77 91

For a more relaxed golfing experience, the Club de Golf Nestares is a great choice. This course is set in a picturesque rural area and offers a more laid-back atmosphere. The course is well-maintained and suitable for golfers of all levels. I enjoyed a leisurely round here, followed by a delicious meal at the club's restaurant.

Address: Barrio Nestares, s/n, 39200 Reinosa, Cantabria, Spain

Phone: +34 942 75 32 77

My Personal Outdoor Adventures in Cantabria

Reflecting on my time in Cantabria, I'm filled with memories of breathtaking landscapes, exhilarating adventures, and moments of pure tranquility. Each outdoor activity offered a unique way to connect with the region's natural beauty and rich culture.

One of my most memorable experiences was hiking the Ruta del Cares in the Picos de Europa National Park. The trail was challenging, but the views were absolutely worth it. Standing at the edge of a cliff, looking down at the turquoise waters of the Cares River far below, I felt a profound sense of awe and appreciation for nature's grandeur. The sense of accomplishment I felt at the end of the hike was incredibly rewarding.

Kayaking on the Sella River was another highlight. The gentle flow of the river made for a relaxing paddle, and the surrounding scenery was stunning. I loved the sense of peace and solitude, broken only by the occasional splash of water or the call of a bird. It was a perfect way to unwind and enjoy the natural beauty of Cantabria at a leisurely pace.

Surfing at Playa de Somo was a thrilling adventure. I had never surfed before, but the friendly instructors at the surf school made the learning process fun and exciting. Catching my first wave was an exhilarating experience, and I quickly became hooked. The beach itself was beautiful, with golden sands and clear blue waters, and I spent many happy hours there, both in and out of the water.

Bird watching in the Marismas de Santoña, Victoria y Joyel Natural Park was a deeply enriching experience. With the help of a knowledgeable guide, I was able to spot a variety of bird species, including some rare ones. The highlight was seeing an osprey dive into the water and emerge with a fish in its talons—a truly spectacular sight. The tranquility of the park, combined with the thrill of spotting rare birds, made for a memorable day.

Cycling the Vía Verde del Pas was a delightful way to explore Cantabria's countryside. The trail was easy to follow and offered beautiful views of the surrounding landscape. I loved the freedom of cycling through the open countryside, stopping at picturesque villages along the way. One of my favorite stops was at a small café in a village, where I enjoyed a delicious homemade pastry and chatted with the friendly locals.

Playing golf at Real Golf de Pedreña was a luxurious experience. The course was challenging but fair, and the stunning views of the Bay of Santander made it even more enjoyable. After a satisfying round of golf, I relaxed at the clubhouse, enjoying a refreshing drink and soaking in the beautiful surroundings.

In conclusion, Cantabria offers a wealth of outdoor activities that cater to all interests and fitness levels. Whether you're an avid hiker, a water sports enthusiast, a keen bird watcher, or a golf lover, you'll find plenty to keep you entertained and engaged. The region's natural beauty, combined with its friendly locals and rich cultural heritage, makes it a perfect destination for outdoor adventures. My time in

Cantabria was filled with unforgettable experiences, and I can't wait to return and explore even more of this beautiful region.

Chapter 5

Cultural Experiences

Cantabria, a region brimming with culture and tradition, offers an immersive experience that is both rich and vibrant. During my time in Cantabria, I was fortunate to dive deeply into its cultural fabric, uncovering layers of history, tradition, and community spirit that left an indelible mark on my heart. Here, I share some of my favorite cultural experiences, each filled with personal anecdotes and practical details to help you make the most of your visit.

Traditional Music and Dance

One of the most captivating aspects of Cantabria is its traditional music and dance, known as Jotas Montañesas. These lively performances are not just entertainment; they are a window into the soul of the region. I remember my first encounter with the jota at a local festival in Santander. The energy was palpable, with dancers in traditional attire, their movements swift and synchronized to the beat of tambourines and castanets.

Experience Location: Various festivals and cultural events across Cantabria

Contact: Tourist Information Office, Plaza Porticada, Santander. Phone: +34 942 203 000

What struck me the most was the community involvement. It wasn't just professional dancers; locals of all ages joined in, creating a joyous and inclusive atmosphere. If you want to experience this firsthand, check out the regular performances at the Centro Cultural Doctor Madrazo in Santander. They often host folk music and dance events, providing a perfect introduction to the traditional jotas.

Centro Cultural Doctor Madrazo

Address: Calle Casimiro Sainz, 5, 39004 Santander

Phone: +34 942 203 006

Local Festivals: Celebrate with the Cantabrians

Cantabria's festivals are a celebration of its rich heritage and community spirit. My absolute favorite was the Fiesta de San Juan in the coastal town of Suances. Celebrated on the night of June 23rd, this festival marks the summer solstice with bonfires, music, and dancing. I vividly remember the magical sight of bonfires lighting up the beach, people dancing around them, and the sky lit up with fireworks. It felt like stepping into a scene from a fairy tale.

Fiesta de San Juan

Location: Suances Beach, Suances

Contact: Ayuntamiento de Suances, Plaza Viares, 39340 Suances. Phone: +34 942 811 811

Another unforgettable experience was the La Vijanera festival in Silió, celebrated on the first Sunday of the year. This ancient carnival is one of the oldest in Spain and features participants dressed in elaborate costumes representing different characters and animals. The procession through the village is both eerie and fascinating, filled with the sounds of cowbells and the sight of masked figures.

La Vijanera

Location: Silió

Contact: Asociación Cultural La Vijanera, Calle del Medio, 39438 Silió. Phone: +34 942 829 566

For a taste of maritime tradition, don't miss the Fiesta de la Virgen del Mar in Santander, held on the last Sunday of May. The procession starts at the church and ends at the sea, where a flower offering is made to the Virgin Mary. The entire event is a beautiful homage to the sea, reflecting Cantabria's deep connection with maritime life.

Fiesta de la Virgen del Mar

Location: Santander

Contact: Parroquia Virgen del Mar, Calle Calvo Sotelo, 39012 Santander. Phone: +34 942 220 217

Art and Craft: Dive into the Culture

Cantabria's artistic heritage is just as rich as its traditions. The region's art is a blend of ancient and contemporary, with influences from its Celtic, Roman, and Medieval pasts. During my visit, I was particularly taken by the works at the Museo de Prehistoria y Arqueología de Cantabria (MUPAC). This museum houses an impressive collection of prehistoric artifacts, including cave paintings from the famous Cueva de Altamira.

Museo de Prehistoria y Arqueología de Cantabria (MUPAC)

Address: Calle Bailén, s/n, 39004 Santander

Phone: +34 942 209 922

Speaking of Altamira, a visit to the Museo Nacional y Centro de Investigación de Altamira is a must. The museum provides a detailed history of the cave paintings and their significance, with a meticulous reproduction of the original cave to preserve the fragile artwork. Walking through the replica cave, I felt a profound connection to our distant ancestors who created these masterpieces.

Museo Nacional y Centro de Investigación de Altamira

Address: Santillana del Mar, 39330 Santillana del Mar

Phone: +34 942 818 005

For contemporary art, the Centro Botín in Santander is an architectural marvel and cultural hub. Designed by the renowned architect Renzo Piano, the center hosts exhibitions, performances, and workshops. I attended a photography exhibition there and was struck by the innovative use of space and light.

Centro Botín

Address: Muelle de Albareda, 39004 Santander

Phone: +34 942 047 147

Handicrafts and Souvenirs: What to Buy and Where

No trip to Cantabria is complete without picking up some local handicrafts. The region is known for its pottery, leather goods, and traditional garments. In the quaint village of Comillas, I stumbled upon a small shop called Cerámica de Comillas, which sells beautifully handcrafted pottery. The intricate designs and vibrant colors make for perfect souvenirs.

Cerámica de Comillas

Address: Calle del Marqués, 11, 39520 Comillas

Phone: +34 942 722 566

In Santillana del Mar, I found a charming store named El Zoco, which specializes in traditional Cantabrian textiles and leather goods. The quality and craftsmanship are exceptional, and the owners are more than happy to share the stories behind their products.

El Zoco

Address: Plaza Mayor, 3, 39330 Santillana del Mar

Phone: +34 942 818 205

If you're interested in jewelry, look for Albarcas de Cantabria, traditional wooden clogs often worn in rural areas. They are beautifully crafted and make unique decorative items. I bought a pair from a local market in Potes and they are now a cherished reminder of my travels.

Albarcas de Cantabria

Location: Markets in Potes and other villages

Contact: Local tourist offices for market schedules

Cantabria's markets are also treasure troves for local products. The Mercado de la Esperanza in Santander is one of my favorites. It's not just a market, but a sensory experience. The fresh produce, local cheeses, cured meats, and handmade crafts give you a true taste of Cantabrian life.

Mercado de la Esperanza

Address: Calle Jesús de Monasterio, s/n, 39010 Santander

Phone: +34 942 203 171

Conclusion

Cantabria is a region that celebrates its past while embracing the present. From traditional music and dance to vibrant local festivals, rich artistic heritage, and unique handicrafts, every corner of Cantabria offers a cultural experience that is both immersive and enlightening. My journey through Cantabria was filled with moments of joy, discovery, and deep connection with its people and traditions.

Whether you are visiting for the first time or returning to explore more, I hope this chapter provides you with the insights and inspiration to dive into the cultural richness of Cantabria. Enjoy your travels, and don't forget to bring a piece of Cantabria back with you, whether it's a handcrafted souvenir or a cherished memory.

Chapter 6

Food and Drink

Exploring Cantabria through its food and drink has been one of the most delightful parts of my travels. The region offers a rich culinary landscape that blends traditional flavors with fresh, local ingredients. In this chapter, I'll take you through the must-try dishes, the best restaurants and cafes, the vibrant farmers' markets, and even how you can learn to cook Cantabrian style.

Traditional Cantabrian Cuisine

Cantabrian cuisine is a celebration of the region's natural bounty, from its fertile valleys to its rugged coastline. One of the most iconic dishes you must try is Cocido Montañés. This hearty stew, made with white beans, cabbage, pork, and sausage, is the ultimate comfort food, especially on a chilly day. I remember having my first bowl at a small restaurant in the Picos de Europa mountains—it was love at first bite.

Another standout is Sobaos Pasiegos, a type of rich, buttery sponge cake that is a perfect companion to a cup of coffee or tea. I first tried it at Casa Olmo, a charming bakery in Selaya known for its delicious pastries.

Casa Olmo

Address: Calle Mayor, 17, 39696 Selaya, Cantabria

Phone: +34 942 590 220

You can't talk about Cantabrian cuisine without mentioning Anchoas de Santoña. These anchovies, preserved in olive oil, are renowned for their delicate flavor. I visited Conservas Emilia in Santoña, where I learned about the meticulous process of preparing these anchovies by hand. The taste is unlike any other—mild, slightly salty, and incredibly fresh.

Conservas Emilia

Address: Calle Serna Occina, 14, 39740 Santoña, Cantabria

Phone: +34 942 662 195

Must-Try Dishes and Drinks

When it comes to must-try dishes, the list in Cantabria is long, but here are a few more that left a lasting impression on me:

Quesada Pasiega: This traditional cheesecake, made from fresh milk, eggs, and sugar, has a unique texture and flavor. I had an amazing slice at La Ermita, a restaurant in the heart of Cantabria.

La Ermita

Address: Barrio La Hermita, 33, 39640 Villacarriedo, Cantabria

Phone: +34 942 591 037

Arroz con Leche: A creamy rice pudding that's often flavored with cinnamon and lemon zest. It's a popular dessert, and the best I had was at Restaurante Zacarías in Santander.

Restaurante Zacarías

Address: Calle Hernán Cortés, 38, 39003 Santander, Cantabria

Phone: +34 942 212 800

Rabas: These crispy fried calamari are a staple in the region, often enjoyed with a cold beer. The Bodega Fuente Dé in Santander serves them perfectly golden and tender.

Bodega Fuente Dé

Address: Calle Peña Herbosa, 21, 39003 Santander, Cantabria

Phone: +34 942 216 750

For drinks, you can't miss out on Orujo, a traditional pomace brandy from the Liébana region. It's strong but smooth, with a rich flavor that warms you up instantly. I visited a small distillery in Potes, Destilerías Siderit, where they gave me a fascinating tour and tasting session.

Destilerías Siderit

Address: Avenida Luis Cuevas, 22, 39570 Potes, Cantabria

Phone: +34 942 736 625

Top Restaurants and Cafes

Cantabria is home to many exceptional dining establishments, each offering a unique take on the region's culinary heritage. Here are some of my favorites:

El Serbal: This Michelin-starred restaurant in Santander offers a modern twist on traditional Cantabrian cuisine. The tasting menu is a culinary journey you won't forget.

El Serbal

Address: Calle Andrés del Río, 7, 39004 Santander, Cantabria

Phone: +34 942 220 444

Cenador de Amós: Another Michelin-starred gem, located in the picturesque village of Villaverde de Pontones. The setting is as exquisite as the food, with dishes that highlight the best local ingredients.

Cenador de Amós

Address: Barrio de Villaverde, 54, 39793 Villaverde de Pontones, Cantabria

Phone: +34 942 507 290

La Casona del Judío: Situated in Santander, this restaurant combines traditional flavors with innovative techniques. The ambiance is cozy and the service impeccable.

La Casona del Judío

Address: Repuente, 20, 39012 Santander, Cantabria

Phone: +34 942 342 726

For a more casual dining experience, I recommend:

Bodega Cigalena: A classic spot in Santander known for its extensive wine list and hearty tapas. The atmosphere is lively and welcoming.

Bodega Cigalena

Address: Calle Daoíz y Velarde, 29, 39003 Santander, Cantabria

Phone: +34 942 216 720

La Taberna del Herrero: Located in Torrelavega, this tavern serves up delicious traditional dishes in a rustic setting. It's a great place to enjoy a relaxed meal with friends.

La Taberna del Herrero

Address: Calle Augusto González Linares, 13, 39300 Torrelavega, Cantabria

Phone: +34 942 801 918

Farmers' Markets: Fresh and Local

Visiting farmers' markets in Cantabria is a feast for the senses. These markets offer a glimpse into the region's agricultural abundance and provide an opportunity to taste and buy fresh, local produce. One of my favorite markets is the Mercado de la Esperanza in Santander. The market, housed in a beautiful historic building, is a bustling hub where you can find everything from fresh fish and meats to fruits, vegetables, and artisanal cheeses.

Mercado de la Esperanza

Address: Plaza de la Esperanza, s/n, 39002 Santander, Cantabria

Phone: +34 942 200 987

Another must-visit is the Mercado de Abastos in Torrelavega. This market is known for its vibrant atmosphere and excellent selection of local products. I enjoyed wandering through the stalls, sampling fresh produce, and chatting with the friendly vendors.

Mercado de Abastos

Address: Calle Serafín Escalante, 19, 39300 Torrelavega, Cantabria

Phone: +34 942 888 888

For a truly local experience, the Sunday Market in Potes is unbeatable. Set against the backdrop of the Picos de Europa, this market offers an array of local goods, including handmade crafts and regional delicacies.

Sunday Market in Potes

Address: Plaza de la Serna, 39570 Potes, Cantabria

Phone: +34 942 730 787

Cooking Classes: Learn to Cook Cantabrian Style

One of the best ways to immerse yourself in Cantabrian culture is by learning to cook its traditional dishes. I took a cooking class at La Casa del Cocinero in Santander, and it was a fantastic experience. The chef, Pedro, was incredibly knowledgeable and passionate about Cantabrian cuisine. We started with a visit to the local market to pick out fresh ingredients, and then we headed back to the kitchen to prepare a variety of dishes. I learned how to make Cocido Montañés, Quesada Pasiega, and even got a few tips on perfecting Rabas.

La Casa del Cocinero

Address: Calle Juan de Herrera, 3, 39002 Santander, Cantabria

Phone: +34 942 230 123

Another excellent option is the Cooking Cantabria classes offered in Santillana del Mar. These classes are held in a charming countryside setting and provide a hands-on experience in creating traditional Cantabrian dishes. The instructors are friendly and offer plenty of insights into the region's culinary traditions.

Cooking Cantabria

Address: Barrio Queveda, 17, 39314 Santillana del Mar, Cantabria

Phone: +34 942 898 456

If you find yourself in Comillas, Cocina Tradicional Cantabria offers a wonderful class that focuses on using seasonal ingredients to create classic Cantabrian dishes. The class is held in a beautiful kitchen overlooking the countryside, making it a memorable experience.

Cocina Tradicional Cantabria

Address: Calle Marqués de Comillas, 10, 39520 Comillas, Cantabria

Phone: +34 942 722 334

Personal Experiences

I remember my first encounter with Cantabrian cuisine vividly. It was at a small seaside restaurant in Suances. The owner, a jovial man named José, recommended I try the Caldereta de Pescado (fish stew). The rich, flavorful broth, filled with fresh fish, shellfish, and a medley of vegetables, was like a warm embrace. I struck up a conversation with José, who shared stories of how his grandmother used to make the stew for the family on Sundays. This personal connection to the food made the meal even more special.

On another trip, I stayed in the picturesque village of Santillana del Mar. One morning, I stumbled upon a tiny bakery where an elderly couple was making fresh Sobaos Pasiegos. The aroma was irresistible, and I ended up buying a whole box. We chatted for a while, and they told me about the history of the pastry and its significance in Cantabrian culture. The simple act of sharing their story added so much depth to the experience.

Every time I visit Cantabria, I make it a point to explore new restaurants and cafes. Each place has its own charm and offers a unique perspective on the region's culinary heritage. Whether it's a high-end Michelin-starred restaurant or a humble tavern, the food is always a reflection of the land and the people who call it home.

In conclusion, Cantabria's food and drink are a true testament to the region's rich cultural heritage and natural bounty. From hearty stews and delicate pastries to fresh seafood and robust wines, there's something to delight every palate. I hope this guide helps you navigate the culinary landscape of Cantabria and inspires you to explore the flavors of this beautiful region. Buen provecho!

Chapter 7

Itineraries and Sample Plans

Weekend Getaway

When I think back on my weekend getaways in Cantabria, I remember a whirlwind of beautiful landscapes, charming towns, and mouth-watering food. The region is perfect for a quick escape from the hustle and bustle of everyday life. Here's my ideal weekend itinerary to help you make the most of your time in this stunning part of Spain.

Day 1: Santander and Santillana del Mar

Start your journey in Santander, the capital of Cantabria. This vibrant city offers a mix of urban excitement and natural beauty. Begin your day with a visit to the Palacio de la Magdalena.

Address: Avenida de la Magdalena, 1, 39005 Santander, Cantabria

Phone: +34 942 20 30 84

This stunning palace, set on a peninsula, offers panoramic views of the Bay of Santander. I spent a lovely morning wandering through the grounds and taking in the sea breeze.

Next, head to the Centro Botín.

Address: Muelle de Albareda, 39004 Santander, Cantabria

Phone: +34 942 04 71 47

This contemporary art center is an architectural marvel and houses some fascinating exhibitions. I particularly enjoyed the rooftop terrace, which provides a fantastic view of the city and the bay.

For lunch, make your way to Barrio Pesquero.

Address: Calle Bonifaz, 25, 39003 Santander, Cantabria

Phone: +34 942 21 17 32

This traditional fishing quarter has incredibly fresh seafood. I had the most delicious plate of grilled sardines, accompanied by a chilled glass of local white wine.

In the afternoon, drive to Santillana del Mar, often called "the town of three lies" because it's neither holy (santo), flat (llana), nor by the sea (mar). Despite this, it's one of the most picturesque towns in Spain. Walk through its cobbled streets and visit the Colegiata de Santa Juliana.

Address: Plaza Mayor, s/n, 39330 Santillana del Mar, Cantabria

Phone: +34 942 81 80 15

This beautiful Romanesque church enchanted me with its medieval ambiance and well-preserved architecture.

Check into a cozy rural inn like Hotel Altamira for the night.

Address: Calle Canton, 1, 39330 Santillana del Mar, Cantabria

Phone: +34 942 81 80 01

The rooms are charmingly rustic, and the service is warm and welcoming. For dinner, enjoy a traditional Cantabrian meal at Casa Cossío, where the cocido montañés (mountain stew) is a must-try.

Address: Plaza Mayor, 12, 39330 Santillana del Mar, Cantabria

Phone: +34 942 81 81 15

Day 2: Comillas and San Vicente de la Barquera

After a hearty breakfast, drive to Comillas, a town known for its remarkable modernist architecture. Your first stop should be El Capricho de Gaudí.

Address: Barrio Sobrellano, s/n, 39520 Comillas, Cantabria

Phone: +34 942 72 03 65

This whimsical villa designed by Antoni Gaudí is a joy to explore with its colorful tiles and imaginative design.

Next, visit the Palacio de Sobrellano.

Address: Calle de Joaquín del Piélago, 1, 39520 Comillas, Cantabria

Phone: +34 942 72 03 00

This neo-Gothic palace is another architectural gem. I found the guided tour to be incredibly informative, providing insight into the region's history and the lives of the aristocracy.

For lunch, head to Restaurante El Remedio, just a short drive away.

Address: Carretera de la Playa de Luaña, s/n, 39527 Ruiloba, Cantabria

Phone: +34 942 72 61 25

The restaurant offers breathtaking views of the coastline and a menu featuring local seafood. The arroz con bogavante (lobster rice) was particularly memorable.

In the afternoon, drive to San Vicente de la Barquera, a picturesque fishing village. Take a leisurely stroll along the harbor and visit the Iglesia de Santa María de los Ángeles.

Address: Barrio La Fuente, 1, 39540 San Vicente de la Barquera, Cantabria

Phone: +34 942 71 50 25

This Gothic church offers a peaceful retreat and stunning views of the surrounding landscape.

End your day with a sunset walk along the beach, and perhaps a dinner at El Pescador, where the seafood paella is a local favorite.

Address: Calle Padre Antonio, 4, 39540 San Vicente de la Barquera, Cantabria

Phone: +34 942 71 52 40

After dinner, drive back to Santander for your final night.

Cultural Immersion

If you're looking to immerse yourself in the rich culture of Cantabria, this itinerary will guide you through some of the region's most significant historical and cultural sites.

Day 1: Santander and El Soplao Cave

Begin your cultural journey in Santander. Start with a visit to the Museo de Prehistoria y Arqueología de Cantabria.

Address: Calle Casimiro Sainz, s/n, 39004 Santander, Cantabria

Phone: +34 942 20 83 00

This museum offers a fascinating insight into the prehistoric and Roman history of the region. I was particularly taken with the collection of Paleolithic art and artifacts.

Next, take a short drive to El Soplao Cave.

Address: 39549 Celis, Rionansa, Cantabria

Phone: +34 902 82 02 82

This cave is renowned for its spectacular geological formations, including eccentric stalactites and stalagmites. The guided tour takes you deep into the cave, revealing a subterranean world that's both eerie and beautiful.

For lunch, drive to Cabezón de la Sal and dine at Restaurante El Cruce.

Address: Avenida Generalísimo, 46, 39500 Cabezón de la Sal, Cantabria

Phone: +34 942 70 00 56

The traditional Cantabrian dishes here are hearty and flavorful. I recommend the fabada (bean stew) – it's comfort food at its best.

In the afternoon, visit the Palacio de Sobrellano in Comillas. This neo-Gothic palace offers a glimpse into the opulent lifestyle of the Spanish aristocracy. The detailed carvings and lush gardens are a testament to the craftsmanship of the period.

End your day with a stroll through the Comillas Old Town, where you can admire the blend of Gothic, Renaissance, and modernist architecture. Check into Abba Comillas Golf Hotel for the night.

Address: Urbanización Rovacías, s/n, 39520 Comillas, Cantabria

Phone: +34 942 72 14 50

Day 2: Santillana del Mar and Altamira Caves

Start your day with a visit to the Altamira Museum.

Address: Santillana del Mar, 39330 Cantabria

Phone: +34 942 81 80 05

The museum and replica of the Altamira Caves offer an incredible look at prehistoric art. The original caves, which are not open to the public, contain some of the most well-preserved cave paintings in the world. The replica is meticulously done and gives you a real sense of the ancient artistry.

Afterward, explore Santillana del Mar. This town is like stepping back in time, with its cobblestone streets and medieval buildings. Visit the Museo Diocesano to see a collection of religious art and artifacts.

Address: Plaza del Abad Francisco Navarro, s/n, 39330 Santillana del Mar, Cantabria

Phone: +34 942 81 80 04

For lunch, dine at La Villa. The restaurant offers a cozy atmosphere and a menu featuring local specialties.

Address: Calle Santo Domingo, 1, 39330 Santillana del Mar, Cantabria

Phone: +34 942 81 81 81

The lechazo (roast lamb) was tender and flavorful. Spend the afternoon visiting the Collegiate Church of Santa Juliana and exploring the small shops and boutiques that line the streets of Santillana del Mar. Don't forget to pick up some local crafts and souvenirs.

Head back to Santander for the night and enjoy a relaxing evening at Gran Hotel Sardinero.

Address: Plaza de Italia, 1, 39005 Santander, Cantabria

Phone: +34 942 27 10 00

Outdoor Adventure

Cantabria's diverse landscapes make it a paradise for outdoor enthusiasts. Here's an itinerary packed with adventure and natural beauty.

Day 1: Picos de Europa and Fuente Dé

Start your adventure with a drive to the Picos de Europa National Park. The stunning mountain scenery is perfect for hiking and exploring. Begin your day at Fuente Dé, where you can take the cable car up to the top.

Address: 39588 Fuente Dé, Cantabria

Phone: +34 942 73 65 05

The views from the top are breathtaking, with rugged peaks and verdant valleys stretching out before you.

Once at the top, there are several hiking trails to choose from. I took the Ruta de los Puertos de Áliva, which offers a moderate hike with stunning views of the mountains and valleys. Don't forget to pack a picnic – there are plenty of beautiful spots to stop and enjoy your lunch.

After a day of hiking, drive to Potes, a charming mountain town. Check into Hotel Valdecoro, a cozy hotel with comfortable rooms and friendly service.

Address: Avenida de España, 20, 39570 Potes, Cantabria

Phone: +34 942 73 80 25

For dinner, head to Restaurante Casa Cayo. The local dishes here are hearty and delicious, perfect after a day of outdoor activities.

Address: Calle San Roque, 3, 39570 Potes, Cantabria

Phone: +34 942 73 80 06

I highly recommend the cocido lebaniego, a traditional stew that's both filling and flavorful.

Day 2: Liébana and River Cares

Start your day with a visit to the Monastery of Santo Toribio de Liébana. This ancient monastery is set in a beautiful valley and offers a peaceful retreat from the world. The guided tour provides fascinating insights into the history and significance of the site.

Address: Calle Santo Toribio, s/n, 39570 Camaleño, Cantabria

Phone: +34 942 73 11 12

Next, drive to Cares Gorge for one of the most spectacular hikes in Spain. The Ruta del Cares is a 12-kilometer trail that runs through the heart of the Picos de Europa, following the Cares River.

Address: Calle Ca-1, 39587 Tresviso, Cantabria

Phone: +34 942 73 95 20

The trail is relatively flat but offers dramatic views of the gorge and the surrounding mountains.

After your hike, return to Potes and enjoy a relaxing evening. Treat yourself to a delicious meal at Asador Llorente, where the grilled meats are a specialty.

Address: Calle Cántabra, 3, 39570 Potes, Cantabria

Phone: +34 942 73 80 55

Family-Friendly Trip

Traveling with family is always an adventure, and Cantabria offers plenty of activities that are fun for all ages. Here's a family-friendly itinerary that combines fun, education, and relaxation.

Day 1: Santander and Cabárceno Nature Park

Begin your family adventure in Santander. Start with a visit to the Maritime Museum of Cantabria. The museum is packed with interactive exhibits that kids will love.

Address: Calle Severiano Ballesteros, s/n, 39004 Santander, Cantabria

Phone: +34 942 27 49 62

My children were fascinated by the aquarium and the models of old ships.

Next, drive to Cabárceno Nature Park. This park is home to over a hundred species of animals living in semi-freedom in a natural environment.

Address: 39793 Obregón, Cantabria

Phone: +34 942 56 36 90

We spent the entire afternoon here, watching elephants, giraffes, and even tigers roam around. There are plenty of picnic areas and restaurants in the park, so pack a lunch or enjoy a meal at one of the cafes.

After a fun-filled day, check into Hotel Chiqui. The hotel is family-friendly with spacious rooms and beautiful views of the beach.

Address: Avenida Manuel García Lago, 9, 39005 Santander, Cantabria

Phone: +34 942 28 06 50

Day 2: Altamira Caves and Santillana del Mar

Start your day with a visit to the Altamira Museum, where the kids can learn about prehistoric art and life. The replica cave is particularly engaging for young minds, sparking their imagination about life thousands of years ago.

Address: Santillana del Mar, 39330 Cantabria

Phone: +34 942 81 80 05

Next, explore Santillana del Mar. The town itself feels like a living museum with its well-preserved medieval buildings. Visit the Zoo and Botanical Garden. The zoo is home to a variety of animals, and the botanical garden is a lovely place for a leisurely walk.

Address: Avenida del Zoo, s/n, 39330 Santillana del Mar, Cantabria

Phone: +34 942 81 80 40

For lunch, stop by La Villa in Santillana del Mar, which offers a kid-friendly menu and a welcoming atmosphere.

Address: Calle Santo Domingo, 1, 39330 Santillana del Mar, Cantabria

Phone: +34 942 81 81 81

In the afternoon, visit the Museo de la Tortura, a museum dedicated to the history of torture. While some exhibits might be a bit intense for younger children, it's a fascinating and educational experience for older kids and adults.

Address: Calle de Santo Domingo, 6, 39330 Santillana del Mar, Cantabria

Phone: +34 942 81 81 20

Return to Santander for the night and enjoy a relaxing evening at the beach or the hotel.

Budget Travel

Traveling on a budget doesn't mean you have to miss out on the best experiences. Cantabria offers plenty of affordable activities and accommodations that won't break the bank.

Day 1: Santander

Start your budget adventure in Santander. The city offers many free or inexpensive activities. Begin with a walk along the Paseo de Pereda, a beautiful promenade along the waterfront. I enjoyed the views of the bay and the elegant buildings lining the street.

Visit the Mercado de la Esperanza, where you can sample local produce and pick up some affordable snacks. The bustling market is a great place to get a feel for local life.

Address: Plaza de la Esperanza, s/n, 39002 Santander, Cantabria

Phone: +34 942 20 30 14

For lunch, grab a bite at Bodega del Riojano. This charming tapas bar offers delicious dishes at reasonable prices. The atmosphere is lively and the food is fresh and flavorful.

Address: Calle del Rio de la Pila, 5, 39003 Santander, Cantabria

Phone: +34 942 21 45 82

In the afternoon, visit the Museum of Modern and Contemporary Art of Santander and Cantabria. The entrance fee is minimal, and the museum houses an impressive collection of contemporary art.

Address: Calle Rubio, 6, 39001 Santander, Cantabria

Phone: +34 942 23 49 28

Check into a budget-friendly hotel like Hostal Jardin Secreto. The rooms are clean and comfortable, and the location is convenient.

Address: Calle del Cardenal Cisneros, 37, 39007 Santander, Cantabria

Phone: +34 942 37 59 01

Day 2: Comillas and San Vicente de la Barquera

Take a bus to Comillas. The town is small enough to explore on foot, and many of its attractions are free or inexpensive. Visit the Plaza del Corro Campios, a lovely square surrounded by historic buildings. The atmosphere is relaxed and charming.

Address: Calle del Corro Campios, 39520 Comillas, Cantabria

Next, head to San Vicente de la Barquera. This fishing village offers stunning views and plenty of opportunities for budget-friendly activities. Walk along the harbor and visit the Iglesia de Santa María de los Ángeles.

Address: Barrio La Fuente, 1, 39540 San Vicente de la Barquera, Cantabria

Phone: +34 942 71 50 25

For lunch, try El Pescador, where you can enjoy fresh seafood without breaking the bank. The menu offers a variety of affordable options, and the quality is excellent.

Address: Calle Padre Antonio, 4, 39540 San Vicente de la Barquera, Cantabria

Phone: +34 942 71 52 40

Spend the afternoon exploring the natural beauty of the area. The beaches are pristine and perfect for a relaxing walk or a picnic.

Return to Santander for your final night and reflect on the incredible experiences you've had without spending a fortune.

Cantabria has so much to offer, whether you're looking for a quick weekend getaway, a deep cultural immersion, an outdoor adventure, a family-friendly trip, or a budget travel experience. Each itinerary provides a unique way to explore this beautiful region, ensuring you leave with unforgettable memories.

Chapter 8

Accommodation

When I first arrived in Cantabria, I was struck by the sheer variety of accommodation options available. Whether you're looking for luxury, budget, or something unique, this beautiful region has it all. Here's a comprehensive guide to help you choose the perfect place to stay.

Overview of Accommodation Options

Cantabria offers a wide range of accommodations to suit every traveler's needs and budget. From opulent resorts overlooking the sea to cozy guesthouses nestled in charming villages, there's something for everyone. My stays in Cantabria have given me the chance to experience a bit of everything, and here are some insights based on my personal experiences.

Luxury Resorts

If you're looking to indulge in some luxury, Cantabria won't disappoint. During one of my trips, I stayed at the magnificent Gran Hotel Sardinero. Located right by the beach in Santander, this hotel offers breathtaking views of the ocean. The rooms are spacious and elegantly decorated, and the service is impeccable. Waking up to the sound of waves and enjoying breakfast on the terrace was one of the highlights of my trip.

Gran Hotel Sardinero

Address: Plaza de Italia, 1, 39005 Santander, Cantabria

Phone: +34 942 271 100

Another luxurious option is the Hotel Real, a historic hotel that exudes old-world charm. The hotel's spa facilities are top-notch, and after a day of exploring, I loved unwinding in the sauna and enjoying a relaxing massage. The panoramic views of the Bay of Santander from the hotel are simply unforgettable.

Hotel Real

Address: Paseo Pérez Galdós, 28, 39005 Santander, Cantabria

Phone: +34 942 291 500

Budget-Friendly Hotels

Traveling on a budget doesn't mean you have to compromise on comfort. Cantabria offers several budget-friendly hotels that provide great value for money. One of my favorite budget stays was at the Hotel Chiqui. This charming hotel is located on the outskirts of Santander, right next to the Sardinero Beach. The rooms are clean and comfortable, and the hotel has a friendly, welcoming atmosphere.

Hotel Chiqui

Address: Av. Manuel García Lago, 9, 39005 Santander, Cantabria

Phone: +34 942 282 700

For those looking to stay in the heart of the city, Hotel San Glorio is a fantastic option. It's conveniently located near the train station, making it easy to explore the region. The rooms are simple but comfortable, and the staff is incredibly helpful with tips on local attractions and dining spots.

Hotel San Glorio

Address: Calle Ruiz Zorrilla, 18, 39009 Santander, Cantabria

Phone: +34 942 222 423

Boutique Guesthouses

If you prefer a more intimate and personalized experience, Cantabria's boutique guesthouses are a perfect choice. During one of my visits, I stayed at Posada La Llosa de Somo. This charming guesthouse is located in the quaint village of Somo, just a short ferry ride from Santander. The rustic decor, warm hospitality, and delicious homemade breakfast made my stay truly memorable.

Posada La Llosa de Somo

Address: Calle Palacio, 11, 39140 Somo, Cantabria

Phone: +34 942 510 375

Another gem is Casona del Judío, a beautifully restored 19th-century mansion in Santander. The guesthouse combines historical charm with modern comforts, and the on-site restaurant serves exquisite local cuisine. I particularly enjoyed relaxing in the garden with a glass of wine after a day of sightseeing.

Casona del Judío

Address: Calle Repuente, 20, 39012 Santander, Cantabria

Phone: +34 942 343 543

Unique Stays

For those seeking a unique and unforgettable experience, Cantabria offers some truly special accommodation options. One of the most unique stays I had was at the Cabárceno Nature Park, where you can stay in rustic cabins surrounded by wildlife. Waking up to the sight of elephants and giraffes roaming freely was a surreal experience.

Cabárceno Nature Park Cabins

Address: Carretera del Parque, s/n, 39627 Cabárceno, Cantabria

Phone: +34 942 563 736

For a taste of traditional Cantabrian life, consider staying in a rural house, or casa rural. I had the pleasure of staying at Casa de las Indianas, a beautifully restored rural house in the village of Selaya. The house is full of character, with antique furniture and a lovely garden. The owner, María, was incredibly welcoming and shared fascinating stories about the history of the house and the region.

Casa de las Indianas

Address: Barrio La Vega, 23, 39696 Selaya, Cantabria

Phone: +34 942 591 068

Top Recommended Hotels and Resorts

Based on my experiences and feedback from fellow travelers, here are some top recommended hotels and resorts in Cantabria:

Gran Hotel Sardinero

Address: Plaza de Italia, 1, 39005 Santander, Cantabria

Phone: +34 942 271 100

Hotel Real

Address: Paseo Pérez Galdós, 28, 39005 Santander, Cantabria

Phone: +34 942 291 500

Hotel Chiqui

Address: Av. Manuel García Lago, 9, 39005 Santander, Cantabria

Phone: +34 942 282 700

Posada La Llosa de Somo

Address: Calle Palacio, 11, 39140 Somo, Cantabria

Phone: +34 942 510 375

Casona del Judío

Address: Calle Repuente, 20, 39012 Santander, Cantabria

Phone: +34 942 343 543

Cabárceno Nature Park Cabins

Address: Carretera del Parque, s/n, 39627 Cabárceno, Cantabria

Phone: +34 942 563 736

Casa de las Indianas

Address: Barrio La Vega, 23, 39696 Selaya, Cantabria

Phone: +34 942 591 068

Choosing the Right Accommodation for You

Choosing the right accommodation depends on your preferences, budget, and the kind of experience you're looking for. Here are some factors to consider:

Location: If you want to explore Santander's vibrant city life, staying in a central hotel like Hotel San Glorio is ideal. For a more tranquil experience, consider staying in a rural house like Casa de las Indianas or a guesthouse in a coastal village like Posada La Llosa de Somo.

Amenities: Think about what amenities are important to you. Luxury resorts like Gran Hotel Sardinero and Hotel Real offer top-notch facilities, including spas, gourmet restaurants, and stunning views. If you prefer a more homely atmosphere, boutique guesthouses provide a cozy and personalized experience.

Budget: Cantabria offers accommodation options for every budget. Budget-friendly hotels like Hotel Chiqui offer great value without compromising on comfort. For a unique experience, rural houses and nature park cabins provide affordable alternatives that are rich in character.

Experience: Consider what kind of experience you want. If you're looking for luxury and relaxation, a high-end resort might be the best choice. For adventure and nature, staying at Cabárceno Nature Park Cabins offers a unique opportunity to be close to wildlife. For cultural immersion, a stay in a traditional rural house or a boutique guesthouse in a historic building can be very rewarding.

Booking Tips and Tricks

Booking your accommodation can sometimes be a daunting task, but here are some tips and tricks that have worked for me:

Book Early: Popular accommodations can fill up quickly, especially during peak travel seasons. I usually book my stays several months in advance to secure the best options and rates.

Check Reviews: Reading reviews from other travelers can provide valuable insights into what to expect. Websites like TripAdvisor and booking platforms often have detailed reviews that highlight the pros and cons of each place.

Consider Direct Booking: Sometimes booking directly through the hotel's website or contacting them via phone can offer better rates or additional perks. For instance, when I booked directly with Posada La Llosa de Somo, I received a complimentary breakfast.

Be Flexible: If your travel dates are flexible, you might find better deals. Mid-week stays are often cheaper than weekends, and visiting during the shoulder seasons (spring and fall) can save you money while avoiding the crowds.

Look for Packages: Some hotels and resorts offer package deals that include meals, spa treatments, or guided tours. These packages can provide excellent value and enhance your stay.

Ask for Recommendations: Don't hesitate to ask locals or the staff at your accommodation for recommendations. They often have insider tips on the best places to eat, hidden gems to visit, and upcoming events.

Consider Location: Proximity to attractions and amenities is crucial. During my stay in Santander, being close to the beach and city center at Gran Hotel Sardinero made exploring the area much more convenient.

Cantabria is a region that offers a wealth of accommodation options to suit every taste and budget. Whether you're seeking luxury, adventure, cultural immersion, or a unique stay, you're sure to find the perfect place to rest and rejuvenate during your visit. My time in Cantabria was enriched by the variety and quality of accommodations I experienced, and I hope this guide helps you find the ideal spot to make your stay just as memorable.

Chapter 9

Practical Tips and Advice

What to Pack for Cantabria

When preparing for a trip to Cantabria, packing the right items can make a significant difference in your comfort and enjoyment. I've visited Cantabria multiple times, and through trial and error, I've learned what works best.

1. Clothing: Cantabria's climate is quite varied. Summers can be warm, but evenings and early mornings are often cool, especially in the coastal areas and mountains. Bring lightweight clothing for the day, but don't forget a warm jacket or sweater for the evenings. In the winter, pack layers and a good waterproof jacket, as it can get quite rainy.

2. Footwear: Comfortable walking shoes are a must. Whether you're exploring the charming streets of

Santander, hiking in the Picos de Europa, or strolling along the beaches, you'll need sturdy, supportive footwear. If you plan on doing any serious hiking, bring appropriate hiking boots.

3. Rain Gear: Cantabria is known for its lush landscapes, which means it can be quite rainy. An umbrella and a lightweight, packable rain jacket are essential. During one of my hikes in the Picos, I was caught in a sudden downpour. My rain jacket saved the day, allowing me to continue enjoying the breathtaking scenery without getting soaked.

4. Beach Gear: If you're visiting in the summer, don't forget your swimsuit, beach towel, and sunscreen. The beaches in Cantabria are beautiful, and you'll want to take full advantage of them. Playa de Somo and Playa de la Magdalena are some of my favorites.

5. Daypack: A small backpack is invaluable for day trips. You can carry water, snacks, a camera, and any other essentials you might need while exploring. I

found it particularly useful when visiting the Altamira Caves and the charming village of Santillana del Mar.

6. Travel Guide and Map: Although digital maps are handy, having a physical map and a travel guide can be useful, especially in areas with limited internet access. I often found myself referring to my guidebook while exploring the smaller, less touristy towns.

Health and Safety Tips

Your health and safety should always be a priority while traveling. Here are some tips based on my experiences in Cantabria:

1. Health Insurance: Make sure you have travel insurance that covers medical expenses. While healthcare in Spain is excellent, having insurance will give you peace of mind. I had a minor mishap while hiking and needed a quick trip to the local clinic in Potes. My insurance covered everything smoothly.

2. Pharmacies: Pharmacies are widely available, and pharmacists in Spain are very knowledgeable. For minor ailments or to purchase over-the-counter medications, just look for a sign with a green cross. In Santander, I visited Farmacia La Sardinera (Phone: +34 942 213 123), and they were incredibly helpful.

3. Emergency Numbers: The emergency number in Spain is 112. Whether you need medical assistance, the fire brigade, or police, this number will connect you to the appropriate service. I recommend saving this number in your phone just in case.

4. Drinking Water: Tap water in Cantabria is safe to drink. Carry a reusable water bottle to stay hydrated, especially if you're out exploring all day.

5. Sun Protection: The sun can be quite strong, even in northern Spain. Always wear sunscreen, sunglasses, and a hat when spending time outdoors. I made the mistake of not reapplying sunscreen during a long beach day at Playa de Langre and ended up with a nasty sunburn.

6. Personal Safety: Cantabria is generally very safe, but it's always wise to take basic precautions. Keep an eye on your belongings, especially in crowded places like markets and festivals. When I attended the Semana Grande in Santander, I used a money belt to keep my valuables secure.

Money Matters: Currency and Budgeting

Managing your finances while traveling can be straightforward if you plan ahead. Here are some tips for handling money in Cantabria:

1. Currency: Spain uses the Euro (€). It's a good idea to carry some cash, especially for smaller purchases or in rural areas where card payments might not be accepted.

2. ATMs: ATMs are widely available in cities and towns. Look for machines affiliated with major banks like Santander or BBVA. I used the ATM at Banco

Santander (Address: Calle Juan de Herrera, 1, 39002 Santander, Phone: +34 942 208 000) frequently and found it reliable.

3. Credit and Debit Cards: Major credit and debit cards are accepted in most establishments. However, it's always good to have some cash on hand for smaller businesses or markets. Inform your bank of your travel plans to avoid any issues with card transactions.

4. Budgeting: Cantabria can be enjoyed on various budgets. For a mid-range budget, you can expect to spend around €60-€100 per day, including accommodation, meals, and activities. Eating out can be very affordable, especially if you opt for the menú del día (daily menu) offered by many restaurants.

5. Tipping: Tipping in Spain is not obligatory but is appreciated. In restaurants, leaving a tip of around 5-10% is customary if the service was good. For taxi drivers and hotel staff, rounding up the fare or leaving a small tip is sufficient.

6. Market Bargains: If you love shopping, check out local markets for unique souvenirs and fresh produce. I had a great time at Mercado del Este (Address: Calle Hernán Cortés, 4, 39003 Santander, Phone: +34 942 228 885), where I found beautiful ceramics and delicious local cheeses.

Etiquette and Local Customs

Understanding local customs can enhance your travel experience and help you connect better with the locals. Here are some etiquette tips for Cantabria:

1. Greetings: A common greeting in Spain is a handshake, or if you are familiar with someone, a kiss on both cheeks. In more formal settings, you can use "Señor" or "Señora" followed by the person's last name.

2. Dining Etiquette: Spanish mealtimes are usually later than what you might be used to. Lunch is typically between 2:00 pm and 3:00 pm, and dinner is

often served after 9:00 pm. When dining out, it's polite to wait until everyone has been served before starting to eat. I enjoyed several leisurely dinners at La Casona del Judío (Address: Calle Repuente, 20, 39012 Santander, Phone: +34 942 344 457), where the service was impeccable, and the food was divine.

3. Dress Code: Spaniards tend to dress more formally than in some other countries. Even when sightseeing, it's common to see locals in smart casual attire. In churches or religious sites, ensure your shoulders and knees are covered.

4. Language: While many people in Cantabria speak English, especially in tourist areas, it's appreciated if you try to speak some Spanish. Simple phrases like "Hola" (Hello), "Gracias" (Thank you), and "Por favor" (Please) go a long way.

5. Respecting Traditions: If you visit during a local festival or religious event, observe and respect the customs. I attended the La Vijanera festival in Silió, which celebrates the arrival of the new year with

elaborate costumes and traditional rituals. Being respectful and asking permission before taking photos made my experience much more positive.

Do's and Don'ts in Cantabria

To ensure you have an enjoyable and respectful experience in Cantabria, here are some do's and don'ts based on my travels:

Do's:

Do explore local cuisine: Cantabria has a rich culinary heritage. Try regional dishes like cocido montañés (mountain stew) and sobao pasiego (a traditional cake). My favorite spot for cocido montañés is Casa Setién (Address: Barrio la Iglesia, 32, 39792 Hoznayo, Phone: +34 942 525 005).

Do visit the natural parks: The Picos de Europa National Park and Cabárceno Natural Park are must-visits. The landscapes are stunning, and the wildlife is abundant. Be sure to bring a camera and plenty of water.

Do take part in local festivals: Festivals are a significant part of Cantabrian culture. Participate in the festivities, enjoy the music, and sample the local food. The Feria de Santiago in Santander is a great event to experience local traditions.

Do respect the environment: Cantabria's natural beauty is one of its greatest assets. Dispose of litter properly, stay on marked trails, and respect wildlife habitats.

Do learn a few Spanish phrases: Locals appreciate it when you make an effort to speak their language. Simple phrases like "¿Dónde está el baño?" (Where is the bathroom?) and "¿Cuánto cuesta?" (How much does it cost?) can be very helpful.

Don'ts:

Don't be loud in public places: Spaniards value a more subdued public demeanor. Keep your voice down in restaurants, on public transport, and in shops.

Don't skip siesta time: Many shops and businesses close in the early afternoon for siesta, usually from 2:00 pm to 5:00 pm. Plan your activities around this, and use the time to relax and recharge.

Don't tip excessively: Tipping is appreciated but not obligatory. A small amount is usually sufficient. Over-tipping can be seen as excessive and is not the norm.

Don't be impatient: Spanish culture has a more relaxed attitude towards time. Meals are meant to be enjoyed leisurely, and services may take longer than you're used to. Embrace the slower pace and enjoy the moment.

Don't ignore local customs: Each region in Spain has its own customs and traditions. Take the time to learn about them and show respect. For example, in

Cantabria, the Fiesta de San Juan is celebrated with bonfires on the beach. Respecting these traditions can lead to a richer travel experience.

Cantabria is a region full of charm, beauty, and tradition. By following these practical tips and advice, you'll be well-prepared to enjoy all that this incredible part of Spain has to offer. Whether you're hiking in the mountains, relaxing on the beaches, or immersing yourself in local culture, Cantabria promises an unforgettable experience. Enjoy your travels!

Chapter 10

Enhancing Your Experience

Guided Tours: Why and How to Choose One

One of the best ways to truly immerse yourself in the rich history and natural beauty of Cantabria is through guided tours. During my time in Cantabria, I found that guided tours provided not only an in-depth understanding of the sights but also personal anecdotes and local legends that made each place come alive.

When choosing a guided tour, consider what interests you most. Are you a history buff, a nature enthusiast, or a foodie? For history enthusiasts, I highly recommend the Santander City Tour. This tour covers the major historical landmarks of the city, including the Palacio de la Magdalena and the Cathedral of Santander. My guide was incredibly knowledgeable and shared fascinating stories about the city's past.

Address: Calle Juan de Herrera, 2, 39002 Santander, Cantabria

Phone: +34 942 20 30 84

For nature lovers, the Picos de Europa National Park Tour is a must. The guides are adept at navigating the rugged terrain and can point out rare flora and fauna. I remember a particularly exhilarating hike through the park where our guide pointed out golden eagles soaring overhead.

Address: Barrio Espinama, s/n, 39588 Camaleño, Cantabria

Phone: +34 942 73 65 05

If you're a foodie like me, the Cantabrian Food and Wine Tour offers a delectable journey through local vineyards and traditional eateries. I still recall the taste of the local blue cheese and the robust flavor of the Cantabrian wines we sampled.

Address: Plaza del Ayuntamiento, 1, 39002 Santander, Cantabria

Phone: +34 942 20 30 00

Best Times to Visit: Seasonal Highlights

Cantabria is beautiful year-round, but each season offers its own unique charm. Here's a breakdown of what to expect and enjoy during each season:

Spring (March to May): Spring is one of my favorite times to visit Cantabria. The countryside is lush and green, and the flowers are in full bloom. The weather is mild, making it perfect for hiking and exploring the outdoors. Spring is also the season for local festivals. I had the chance to experience the Fiestas de la Primavera in Santander, a lively celebration with parades, music, and traditional dances.

Summer (June to August): Summer is the peak tourist season, with warm temperatures ideal for beach activities. The beaches of Santander, such as El Sardinero, are perfect for sunbathing and swimming. I spent many afternoons lounging on the soft sand, the sound of the waves providing a soothing backdrop.

Address: Calle Joaquín Costa, s/n, 39005 Santander, Cantabria

Phone: +34 942 27 10 00

Autumn (September to November): Autumn brings cooler temperatures and a burst of fall colors. It's an excellent time for hiking in the Picos de Europa and exploring the picturesque villages. I particularly enjoyed visiting the Valley of Liébana during this season, where the vineyards were vibrant with autumn hues.

Address: Calle Santo Toribio, s/n, 39570 Camaleño, Cantabria

Phone: +34 942 73 11 12

Winter (December to February): Winter is the off-peak season but still holds its own charm. The coastal areas remain relatively mild, and the mountainous regions often get a dusting of snow, creating a beautiful winter landscape. I spent a cozy winter weekend in the town of Potes, enjoying the local cuisine and the peaceful atmosphere.

Address: Avenida de España, 20, 39570 Potes, Cantabria

Phone: +34 942 73 80 25

Photography Tips: Capturing the Beauty of Cantabria

As an avid photographer, I found Cantabria to be a treasure trove of stunning photo opportunities. Here are some tips to help you capture its beauty:

Golden Hour: The best time to take photos is during the golden hour, just after sunrise and before sunset. The soft, warm light adds a magical quality to your photos. I captured some of my favorite shots at Playa de los Locos in Suances during this time, with the sun casting a golden glow over the cliffs.

Address: Barrio Playa, 39340 Suances, Cantabria

Phone: +34 942 81 00 01

Perspective: Don't be afraid to experiment with different angles and perspectives. When I visited the Cueva El Soplao, I found that shooting from a low angle highlighted the dramatic stalactites and stalagmites.

Address: 39549 Celis, Rionansa, Cantabria

Phone: +34 902 82 02 82

Local Life: Capturing everyday moments of local life can add a rich dimension to your travel photos. Markets, street performers, and traditional festivals provide excellent opportunities. The Mercado de la Esperanza in Santander is bustling with activity and vibrant colors, making it a perfect subject.

Address: Plaza de la Esperanza, s/n, 39002 Santander, Cantabria

Phone: +34 942 20 30 14

Nature: Cantabria's natural beauty is best captured in wide shots that showcase its expansive landscapes.

Use a wide-angle lens to capture the sweeping vistas of the Picos de Europa or the serene beauty of the Saja-Besaya Natural Park.

Address: Barrio La Molina, s/n, 39409 Los Tojos, Cantabria

Phone: +34 942 04 94 38

Day Trips to Nearby Attractions

Cantabria's central location makes it an excellent base for day trips to nearby attractions. Here are a few of my favorites:

Bilbao: Just a short drive away, Bilbao is famous for the Guggenheim Museum. The museum's modern architecture and impressive art collection make it a must-visit.

Address: Avenida Abandoibarra, 2, 48009 Bilbao, Vizcaya

Phone: +34 944 35 90 00

San Sebastián: Known for its beautiful beaches and culinary scene, San Sebastián is perfect for a day of exploration. I spent a delightful afternoon walking along the La Concha Beach and enjoying pintxos in the old town.

Address: Kontxa Pasealekua, s/n, 20007 Donostia, Gipuzkoa

Phone: +34 943 48 11 66

Valles Pasiegos: This area is famous for its rolling hills and traditional Pasiego houses. It's a great place to experience rural life in Cantabria. I enjoyed a scenic drive through the valleys and stopped at several charming villages along the way.

Santillana del Mar: Although I've mentioned it before, it's worth noting that this town is perfect for a day trip if you're based in Santander. The town's medieval charm and the nearby Altamira Caves make it a must-see.

How to Make Friends with Locals

One of the most enriching aspects of travel is connecting with the locals. During my time in Cantabria, I found several ways to make friends and immerse myself in the local culture.

Learn Some Spanish: Even a basic understanding of Spanish can go a long way in breaking the ice. The locals appreciate the effort, and it often leads to more meaningful interactions. I took a few Spanish classes before my trip, which helped immensely.

Join Local Events: Participating in local events and festivals is a great way to meet people. I attended the Fiestas de la Virgen del Mar in Santander, and the lively atmosphere made it easy to strike up conversations with fellow attendees.

Visit Local Markets: Markets are social hubs where you can chat with vendors and shoppers. I had many delightful conversations at the Mercado de la Esperanza in Santander. Asking for recommendations on local delicacies is a great conversation starter.

Stay in Local Accommodations: Choosing to stay in family-run inns or bed and breakfasts instead of large hotels can provide more opportunities for interaction. During my stay at Hotel Altamira in Santillana del Mar, the owners were incredibly welcoming and shared lots of local tips and stories.

Address: Calle Canton, 1, 39330 Santillana del Mar, Cantabria

Phone: +34 942 81 80 01

Take Part in Guided Tours: Local guides often share personal stories and insights that you wouldn't get from a guidebook. I found that after a tour, it's easy to continue the conversation and ask for additional recommendations.

Be Open and Friendly: Sometimes, making friends is as simple as being open to new experiences and friendly in your interactions. Whether I was ordering food at a café, shopping for souvenirs, or asking for directions, a smile and a friendly attitude always opened doors.

Enhancing your experience in Cantabria involves more than just visiting the sights. It's about immersing yourself in the local culture, making connections, and discovering the hidden gems that make this region so special. Whether you're joining a guided tour, capturing the beauty of the landscape through your lens, or making new friends, each experience adds a rich layer to your journey. Enjoy your travels and cherish every moment in this beautiful part of Spain.

Chapter 11

Family Travel Tips

Exploring Cantabria with my family has been one of the most enriching experiences of my life. The region's blend of natural beauty, cultural richness, and warm hospitality makes it an ideal destination for families. From the rugged coastline to the lush mountains, there's something here for everyone, including our little ones. Here's a detailed guide to help you make the most of your family trip to Cantabria.

Activities for Kids

Exploring Nature at Cabárceno Nature Park

One of the first places we visited was the Cabárceno Nature Park. It's more than just a zoo—it's a conservation project where animals live in semi-free conditions. My kids were absolutely thrilled to see elephants, gorillas, and even tigers up close. We spent the entire day there, taking a safari-style tour that allowed us to observe the animals in expansive, naturalistic settings.

Address: Cabárceno Nature Park, 39627 Cabárceno, Cantabria

Phone: +34 902 210 112

Beach Day at Playa de La Magdalena

For a fun and relaxing day, head to Playa de La Magdalena in Santander. This beach is perfect for families with its gentle waves and clean, golden sand. My kids loved building sandcastles and splashing in the shallow water. There are also playgrounds and shaded picnic areas where we could rest and enjoy our packed lunch.

Address: Playa de La Magdalena, Santander, Cantabria

Phone: +34 942 203 000

Interactive Learning at the Maritime Museum of Cantabria

The Maritime Museum of Cantabria is another fantastic spot. It's both educational and entertaining, with interactive exhibits about the region's maritime history. My children were fascinated by the life-sized ship models and the aquariums filled with local marine life. It was a great way to spend an afternoon, combining fun with learning.

Address: San Martín de Bajamar s/n, 39004 Santander, Cantabria

Phone: +34 942 274 962

Adventure at the Forest of Sequoias

For an outdoor adventure, visit the Forest of Sequoias in Cabezón de la Sal. Walking through the towering trees made us feel like we had stepped into another world. The kids enjoyed the easy hiking trails, and we all marveled at the enormous sequoias, some of which are over 100 years old.

Address: Monte Cabezón, 39500 Cabezón de la Sal, Cantabria

Phone: +34 942 701 178

Educational Fun at Altamira Museum and Caves

Another highlight was the Altamira Museum and Caves. Known for the prehistoric cave paintings, the site offers a fascinating glimpse into early human life. The museum has a replica of the original cave, which is closed to preserve the artwork. The exhibits are very child-friendly, with activities designed to engage young minds.

Address: Avda. Marcelino Sanz de Sautuola s/n, 39330 Santillana del Mar, Cantabria

Phone: +34 942 818 005

Family-Friendly Restaurants

Restaurante La Dársena

Finding restaurants that cater to children can sometimes be challenging, but Restaurante La Dársena in Santander was perfect. They offer a diverse menu with plenty of kid-friendly options. The staff was incredibly welcoming and even provided coloring books to keep the kids entertained while we waited for our food. The seafood here is outstanding, and the atmosphere is relaxed and family-oriented.

Address: Calle de Castelar, 19, 39004 Santander, Cantabria

Phone: +34 942 212 450

Mesón El Cucharón

In Santillana del Mar, we stumbled upon Mesón El Cucharón, a cozy restaurant that serves traditional Cantabrian dishes. The children's menu featured smaller portions of local favorites, which was great for introducing my kids to new flavors. The decor is rustic and charming, making it a comfortable place for a family meal.

Address: Plaza Mayor, 6, 39330 Santillana del Mar, Cantabria

Phone: +34 942 818 497

El Pericote de Tanos

In Torrelavega, El Pericote de Tanos offered a warm and inviting atmosphere. The restaurant's patio is perfect for families, with plenty of space for kids to move around. The menu includes a variety of dishes, from hearty stews to fresh salads, ensuring that everyone finds something they like. My kids particularly enjoyed the homemade desserts.

Address: Barrio San Gil, 1, 39300 Torrelavega, Cantabria

Phone: +34 942 883 838

Marucho

For a seaside dining experience, Marucho in Santander is unbeatable. This family-run restaurant specializes in seafood and has a relaxed, welcoming vibe. The kids loved the grilled fish, and the adults appreciated the fresh shellfish. The staff made us feel right at home, and the view of the marina added a special touch to our meal.

Address: Calle Hernán Cortés, 38, 39003 Santander, Cantabria

Phone: +34 942 211 066

La Casona del Judío

If you're looking for a more upscale dining experience that still caters to families, La Casona del Judío in Santander is an excellent choice. The elegant setting and refined menu make it a special treat, but the staff goes out of their way to accommodate children. They offer a kids' menu and are happy to adjust dishes to suit younger palates.

Address: Calle Repuente, 20, 39012 Santander, Cantabria

Phone: +34 942 342 726

Safety Tips for Families

Traveling with kids requires a bit of extra planning to ensure everyone stays safe and happy. Here are some tips based on our experiences in Cantabria:

Stay Hydrated and Protected from the Sun

The Cantabrian climate can be quite varied, but it's important to stay hydrated and protected from the sun, especially during the summer months. Always carry water bottles and encourage your kids to drink frequently. Use sunscreen liberally and reapply throughout the day, particularly if you're spending time outdoors or at the beach.

Keep an Eye on the Kids

Many attractions in Cantabria are family-friendly, but it's still crucial to keep an eye on your children, especially in crowded places or near water. At the beach, always supervise swimming and ensure that they stay within safe areas. At parks and museums, establish a meeting point in case anyone gets separated.

Pack Snacks and Essentials

Having snacks and essential items on hand can make a big difference. We always packed a small backpack with healthy snacks, wet wipes, hand sanitizer, and a first aid kit. These items came in handy during long days of sightseeing and prevented any meltdowns due to hunger or minor injuries.

Use Public Transport Wisely

Public transport in Cantabria is generally safe and reliable. When using buses or trains, keep your children close and ensure they understand the importance of staying near you. We found that traveling during off-peak hours made for a more comfortable and less stressful experience.

Plan Ahead for Activities

While spontaneous adventures can be fun, we found that planning ahead made our trips smoother. Researching opening hours, ticket requirements, and the best times to visit attractions helped us avoid long waits and closed doors. Booking tickets in advance for popular sites like Cabárceno Nature Park saved us time and hassle.

Stay in Family-Friendly Accommodations

Choosing the right place to stay can significantly impact your trip. Look for accommodations that offer family-friendly amenities such as cribs, high chairs, and spacious rooms. We stayed at Hotel Bahía in Santander, which provided a comfortable and convenient base for our explorations.

Address: Calle Cádiz, 22, 39002 Santander, Cantabria

Phone: +34 942 205 000

Engage Kids with Interactive Experiences

Kids tend to get the most out of interactive and hands-on experiences. Museums like the Maritime Museum of Cantabria and outdoor activities at Cabárceno Nature Park kept our children engaged and excited. Look for opportunities where they can touch, explore, and actively participate.

Respect Local Customs and Etiquette

Teaching your children about local customs and etiquette is a great way to prepare them for travel and ensure respectful interactions. For instance, understanding basic Spanish phrases, greeting people politely, and being aware of dining customs can enhance your family's travel experience and make a positive impression.

Emergency Contacts and Local Information

It's always wise to have a list of emergency contacts and local information. This includes knowing the nearest hospital, police station, and pharmacy. Here are a few useful contacts:

Hospital Universitario Marqués de Valdecilla

Address: Avda. Valdecilla, 25, 39008 Santander, Cantabria

Phone: +34 942 202 520

Local Police Station (Comisaría Local de Policía)

Address: Calle Castilla, 10, 39002 Santander, Cantabria

Phone: +34 942 205 200

Pharmacy (Farmacia)

Address: Calle Juan de Herrera, 4, 39002 Santander, Cantabria

Phone: +34 942 216 256

Traveling through Cantabria with my family has provided us with countless unforgettable moments. From exploring nature and history to enjoying local cuisine, every day brought new adventures. With a bit of preparation and these tips in mind, your family is sure to have a fantastic and safe journey in this beautiful region of Spain. Enjoy your travels, and make wonderful memories!

Chapter 12

Solo Travel

Traveling solo can be an incredibly rewarding experience, and Cantabria is one of those places where you feel right at home, even when you're exploring on your own. I've spent several solo trips wandering through this beautiful region, and each time I've found new reasons to fall in love with its landscapes, culture, and people.

Why Cantabria is Perfect for Solo Travelers

One of the first things I noticed about Cantabria is its welcoming atmosphere. Whether you're in the bustling streets of Santander or the serene hills of the Picos de Europa, there's a genuine friendliness that makes solo travelers feel at ease. The locals are warm and often go out of their way to help you, making it an ideal destination if you're traveling alone for the first time.

I remember my first visit to Santander, the region's capital. I stayed at Hotel Bahía, a centrally located hotel with stunning views of the bay. The staff were incredibly helpful, providing tips on places to visit and even helping me book a day trip to the Cabárceno Natural Park.

Hotel Bahía

Address: Calle Cádiz, 22, 39002 Santander

Phone: +34 942 205 000

Another reason Cantabria is great for solo travelers is its manageable size. It's easy to navigate, whether you're using public transportation, renting a car, or even biking. The region offers a perfect blend of urban and rural experiences. In one day, you can explore the historic streets of Santillana del Mar and then hike in the lush valleys of Liébana.

Safety Tips for Solo Travelers

Safety is a priority when traveling alone, and Cantabria is one of the safest regions I've traveled to. However, it's always good to take precautions:

Stay Connected: Make sure your phone is charged and you have local emergency numbers saved. I always carry a portable charger, just in case.

Inform Someone: Let someone know your itinerary. It could be the hotel staff, a friend, or family back home. When I hiked in the Picos de Europa, I left my plans with the reception at Parador de Fuente Dé. They appreciated it and even gave me additional safety tips for the trail.

Parador de Fuente Dé

Address: Fuente Dé, s/n, 39588 Fuente Dé, Camaleño

Phone: +34 942 736 651

Blend In: Try not to look too much like a tourist. Dress like the locals and avoid flashy accessories. This helps you feel more integrated and less of a target for petty theft.

Stay in Well-Lit Areas: Especially at night, stick to well-lit and populated areas. In Santander, I felt completely safe wandering around Paseo de Pereda and Plaza Porticada even after dark.

Trust Your Instincts: If something doesn't feel right, trust your gut and remove yourself from the situation. Cantabria is generally very safe, but it's always better to be cautious.

Best Activities for Solo Travelers

Cantabria offers a wealth of activities that are perfect for solo travelers. Here are some of my top recommendations, based on my personal experiences:

1. Exploring Santander

Santander is a delightful city with a mix of cultural sites, beautiful beaches, and vibrant nightlife. Start your day with a visit to the Centro Botín, an art center designed by Renzo Piano. The contemporary art exhibits are fascinating, and the architecture itself is a sight to behold.

Centro Botín

Address: Muelle de Albareda, s/n, Jardines de Pereda, 39004 Santander

Phone: +34 942 047 147

Afterward, take a leisurely walk along the Paseo de Pereda. This promenade offers stunning views of the bay and is perfect for a relaxing stroll. Don't miss the Palacio de la Magdalena, located on the Magdalena Peninsula. This historic palace was once the summer residence of Spanish royalty, and its gardens and views are simply breathtaking.

Palacio de la Magdalena

Address: Avenida de la Magdalena, s/n, 39005 Santander

Phone: +34 942 203 084

2. Hiking in the Picos de Europa

For nature lovers, the Picos de Europa National Park is a must-visit. The park offers a range of hiking trails suitable for all levels. One of my favorite hikes is the trail to Lagos de Covadonga. The lakes are stunningly beautiful, and the surrounding scenery is awe-inspiring.

On one solo hike, I stayed at the Hostería Peña Sagra in the nearby town of Potes. The owners were friendly and knowledgeable about the best trails, and their advice was invaluable.

Hostería Peña Sagra

Address: Avenida Luis Cuevas, 36, 39570 Potes

Phone: +34 942 730 020

3. Visiting Santillana del Mar

Santillana del Mar is often referred to as the "town of three lies" because it's neither a saint (santo), flat (llana), nor by the sea (mar). However, it is incredibly charming and well worth a visit. Walking through its cobbled streets feels like stepping back in time.

The Collegiate Church of Santa Juliana is the town's most significant monument and an excellent spot for some peaceful reflection. I spent hours just wandering through the medieval streets, visiting small shops, and sampling local pastries.

Collegiate Church of Santa Juliana

Address: Plaza de las Arenas, s/n, 39330 Santillana del Mar

Phone: +34 942 818 815

4. Exploring the Cave Art

Cantabria is famous for its prehistoric cave art, and a visit to the Altamira Cave is a journey back to the origins of human creativity. The real cave is closed to preserve the artwork, but the museum and the replica cave are incredibly well done and provide a fascinating glimpse into prehistoric life.

Altamira Museum

Address: Avenida Marcelino Sanz de Sautuola, s/n, 39330 Santillana del Mar

Phone: +34 942 818 005

5. Relaxing in Comillas

Comillas is a picturesque coastal town with stunning architecture. El Capricho de Gaudí is a whimsical building designed by the famous architect Antoni Gaudí and is one of the highlights of the town. The combination of beach and architectural beauty makes Comillas a great spot for solo travelers looking to unwind.

El Capricho de Gaudí

Address: Barrio Sobrellano, s/n, 39520 Comillas

Phone: +34 942 720 365

6. Enjoying Local Cuisine

One of the best parts of traveling solo is the freedom to indulge in local cuisine whenever you please.

Cantabria's gastronomy is rich and varied. I had one of my best meals at La Casona del Judío in Santander. The chef's tasting menu was a delightful journey through Cantabrian flavors.

La Casona del Judío

Address: Repuente, 20, 39012 Santander

Phone: +34 942 342 726

For a more casual meal, try Bar Restaurante Casa Cossío in Potes. Their cocido lebaniego, a traditional stew, is hearty and delicious.

Bar Restaurante Casa Cossío

Address: Calle Cántabra, 1, 39570 Potes

Phone: +34 942 730 001

7. Taking a Ferry to Somo

For a unique experience, take a ferry from Santander to the small town of Somo. The ferry ride itself offers beautiful views of the Santander skyline and the bay. Once in Somo, you can enjoy the beach or take a surfing lesson. I rented a bike and explored the town and nearby areas, which was both relaxing and invigorating.

Santander Ferry Terminal

Address: Muelle Calderón, s/n, 39002 Santander

Phone: +34 942 203 908

8. Attending a Local Festival

If your visit coincides with one of Cantabria's many festivals, be sure to participate. The Fiestas de la Virgen Grande in Torrelavega are particularly vibrant, with parades, music, and traditional dances. It's a great way to experience the local culture and meet people.

Tourist Information Office Torrelavega

Address: Calle de José María Pereda, 47, 39300 Torrelavega

Phone: +34 942 884 092

Traveling solo in Cantabria has been one of the most fulfilling experiences of my life. The region's natural beauty, rich history, and warm hospitality make it an ideal destination for those seeking both adventure and tranquility. Whether you're exploring bustling cities or peaceful villages, hiking through lush landscapes, or savoring local delicacies, Cantabria offers something for every solo traveler. Enjoy your journey, and may it be as enriching and memorable as mine.

Chapter 13

Romantic Getaways

Top Romantic Spots

Cantabria is an absolute dream for couples looking for a romantic escape. The blend of stunning landscapes, charming villages, and rich cultural heritage creates a perfect backdrop for romance. Let me share some of the top romantic spots that my partner and I discovered during our unforgettable trip.

Santillana del Mar

Address: 39330 Santillana del Mar, Cantabria

Walking through the cobblestone streets of Santillana del Mar felt like stepping back in time. This medieval town is incredibly well-preserved and exudes an old-world charm that's perfect for a romantic stroll. My partner and I wandered hand-in-hand, exploring hidden courtyards and admiring the ancient stone buildings. The highlight was visiting the Collegiate

Church of Santa Juliana, where the serene ambiance added to the romantic atmosphere.

Address: Plaza Mayor, s/n, 39330 Santillana del Mar, Cantabria

Phone: +34 942 81 80 15

Cabo Mayor Lighthouse

Address: Avenida del Faro, s/n, 39012 Santander, Cantabria

Phone: +34 942 20 31 41

The Cabo Mayor Lighthouse in Santander is another spot that's perfect for romance. We went there for a sunset, and the view was simply breathtaking. Watching the sun dip below the horizon, casting golden hues over the rugged coastline, was an experience we'll never forget. The sound of the waves crashing against the cliffs and the gentle sea breeze made it a magical moment.

Playa de Langre

Address: 39160 Langre, Cantabria

For a more secluded and intimate setting, Playa de Langre is ideal. This hidden gem is a pristine beach surrounded by high cliffs. It's less crowded than other beaches, offering a sense of privacy. We spent a lazy afternoon here, lounging on the soft sand and enjoying the serene beauty. The water was crystal clear, and we even took a dip together, feeling like we had our own private paradise.

Comillas

Address: 39520 Comillas, Cantabria

Comillas is a town that combines historical charm with beautiful scenery. We visited El Capricho de Gaudí, a unique and whimsical villa designed by Antoni Gaudí. The colorful tiles and imaginative architecture made it feel like a fairytale setting. Afterward, we explored the town, stopping by quaint cafes and enjoying the picturesque views of the coastline.

Address: Barrio Sobrellano, s/n, 39520 Comillas, Cantabria

Phone: +34 942 72 03 65

Romantic Activities for Couples

Cantabria offers a variety of activities that are perfect for couples looking to create special memories together. Here are some of our favorite romantic activities.

Hot Air Balloon Ride

Address: Carretera Puente Viesgo, s/n, 39670 Puente Viesgo, Cantabria

Phone: +34 942 59 80 03

One of the most memorable experiences we had was a hot air balloon ride over the beautiful landscapes of Cantabria. We booked our ride through a company in Puente Viesgo, and it was worth every penny. Floating high above the rolling hills, lush valleys, and picturesque villages was incredibly romantic. We even shared a champagne toast as we marveled at the stunning views.

Spa Day at Balneario de Puente Viesgo

Address: Calle Manuel Pérez Mazo, s/n, 39670 Puente Viesgo, Cantabria

Phone: +34 942 59 80 61

Speaking of Puente Viesgo, the Balneario de Puente Viesgo is a wonderful place for a relaxing spa day. The thermal baths and massage treatments were a perfect way to unwind and enjoy each other's company. The setting is serene and beautiful, surrounded by nature. We left feeling rejuvenated and even more connected.

Wine Tasting in Picos de Cabariezo

Address: Calle Real, 25, 39574 Cabezon de Liebana, Cantabria

Phone: +34 942 73 50 06

A wine tasting tour in the Picos de Cabariezo region was another highlight. We visited a family-run winery where we learned about the wine-making process and sampled some exquisite local wines. The vineyard was set against a backdrop of rolling hills and lush greenery, making it a perfect spot for a romantic afternoon. We bought a couple of bottles to take home, each sip reminding us of our beautiful day.

Boat Ride in Santander Bay

Address: Paseo de Pereda, s/n, 39004 Santander, Cantabria

Phone: +34 942 21 60 06

A boat ride in Santander Bay was a fantastic way to see the city from a different perspective. We booked a private tour, which allowed us to relax and enjoy the scenery in peace. The coastline, with its beaches and cliffs, looked stunning from the water. The gentle rocking of the boat and the fresh sea air made it a wonderfully romantic experience.

Best Restaurants for a Romantic Dinner

No romantic getaway is complete without indulging in some exquisite dining experiences. Cantabria has a plethora of restaurants that offer delicious food in a romantic setting. Here are some of our top picks for a memorable dinner.

El Serbal

Address: Calle Andrés del Río, 7, 39004 Santander, Cantabria

Phone: +34 942 22 25 15

For a special evening, El Serbal in Santander is a fantastic choice. This Michelin-starred restaurant offers an exceptional dining experience with a focus on local ingredients and creative dishes. The intimate ambiance and impeccable service made our dinner here truly unforgettable. The tasting menu was a culinary journey, each course paired with exquisite wines.

La Casona del Judío

Address: Calle Repuente, 20, 39012 Santander, Cantabria

Phone: +34 942 34 07 47

La Casona del Judío is another gem in Santander. The restaurant is set in a beautiful old house with a charming garden. We dined on the terrace under twinkling fairy lights, which created a magical atmosphere. The menu features a mix of traditional and modern dishes, all beautifully presented. The slow-cooked lamb was a standout dish, tender and full of flavor.

Restaurante Cenador de Amós

Address: Barrio San Martín, 39650 Villaverde de Pontones, Cantabria

Phone: +34 942 50 82 43

Cenador de Amós in Villaverde de Pontones offers a dining experience that's hard to beat. The restaurant is housed in a stunning 18th-century palace, and the setting is incredibly romantic. We chose the tasting menu, which showcased the best of Cantabrian cuisine. Each dish was a work of art, and the flavors were out of this world. The service was attentive and made us feel like royalty.

Casa Lita

Address: Paseo de Pereda, 37, 39004 Santander, Cantabria

Phone: +34 942 22 12 12

For a more casual yet equally romantic dinner, Casa Lita in Santander is perfect. This tapas bar has a lively atmosphere and a great selection of pintxos. We enjoyed a variety of small dishes, each more delicious than the last. Sitting at a table overlooking the bay, we watched the world go by and savored the flavors of Cantabria.

Restaurante Solana

Address: Barrio La Bien Aparecida, 49, 39849 Ampuero, Cantabria

Phone: +34 942 62 32 28

In Ampuero, Restaurante Solana offers a unique dining experience with its blend of traditional and modern cuisine. The restaurant is set in a beautiful rural location, which adds to the romantic ambiance. We dined on the terrace, surrounded by nature, and enjoyed a delicious meal paired with local wines. The staff were welcoming and made our evening special.

Cantabria is a wonderful destination for couples looking for a romantic getaway. Whether you're exploring charming towns, enjoying breathtaking views, indulging in relaxing activities, or dining in exquisite restaurants, every moment is filled with romance. Our time in Cantabria was truly magical, and I hope this chapter helps you create your own unforgettable memories in this beautiful region.

Chapter 14

Nightlife in Cantabria

Cantabria might be famous for its stunning landscapes and rich history, but let me tell you, the nightlife here is equally vibrant and exciting. Whether you're into cozy bars with a laid-back atmosphere, energetic clubs where you can dance the night away, or live music venues where you can experience local talent, Cantabria has something for everyone. Having spent several nights exploring the nightlife in Cantabria, I've gathered some of the best spots and activities to ensure you have an unforgettable evening.

Best Bars and Clubs

One of my favorite bars in Cantabria is Pub Canalla in Santander. This place has a great mix of locals and tourists, and the atmosphere is always lively. The bartenders are friendly and make a mean gin and tonic. The music is a blend of contemporary hits and classic rock, perfect for those nights when you just want to unwind and enjoy good company.

Pub Canalla

Address: Calle del Sol, 20, 39003 Santander, Cantabria

Phone: +34 942 217 012

Another gem is El Divino, a stylish club in Santander. If you're looking for a place to dress up and dance, this is it. The club features a large dance floor, VIP areas, and a rooftop terrace with stunning views of the city. I remember spending a night here with friends, dancing until the early hours, and enjoying the electric atmosphere.

El Divino

Address: Calle Hernán Cortés, 35, 39003 Santander, Cantabria

Phone: +34 942 213 233

For a more relaxed vibe, head to Café Bar El Hombre Pez in Liérganes. This bar is known for its quirky decor and laid-back atmosphere. It's a great spot to enjoy a quiet drink and chat with friends. The owner, Juan, is always up for a conversation and can give you some insider tips about the area.

Café Bar El Hombre Pez

Address: Calle Puente Mayor, 12, 39722 Liérganes, Cantabria

Phone: +34 942 528 173

Live Music Venues

If live music is your thing, Cantabria won't disappoint. One of the best venues I've been to is Sala Black Bird in Santander. This place hosts a variety of live performances, from rock bands to indie artists. The acoustics are fantastic, and the atmosphere is intimate, making it a perfect spot to enjoy live music.

Sala Black Bird

Address: Calle Vista Alegre, 13, 39001 Santander, Cantabria

Phone: +34 942 216 452

Another must-visit is Sala Niágara, also in Santander. This venue has a cool, underground vibe and hosts everything from local bands to international acts. The crowd here is passionate about music, and the energy is infectious. I've seen some incredible performances here that left me buzzing for days.

Sala Niágara

Address: Calle San Simón, 14, 39003 Santander, Cantabria

Phone: +34 942 036 872

For a more traditional experience, check out La Bodega del Riojano. This historic bar and restaurant often features live traditional Spanish music. The setting is cozy, with wooden beams and wine barrels adding to the rustic charm. Enjoying a glass of local wine while listening to flamenco or other regional music here is a memorable experience.

La Bodega del Riojano

Address: Calle del Rio de la Pila, 5, 39003 Santander, Cantabria

Phone: +34 942 216 750

Nighttime Activities

Cantabria offers more than just bars and clubs for nighttime fun. One of the highlights of my trips has been the Santander Night Market. Held during the summer months, this market is a lively hub of activity with stalls selling local crafts, food, and drinks. The market often features live music and street performers, making it a great place to soak up the local culture and enjoy a relaxed evening.

Santander Night Market

Address: Plaza Pombo, 39004 Santander, Cantabria

Phone: +34 942 200 600 (Tourist Information)

If you're up for some adventure, night kayaking on the Bay of Santander is an incredible experience. Paddling under the stars, with the city lights reflecting on the water, is serene and exhilarating at the same time. Several companies offer guided tours, providing all the equipment and safety instructions you need.

Night Kayaking Tours

Contact: Canoe Santander

Phone: +34 608 645 098

For a more laid-back evening, stargazing in the Picos de Europa is a must. The clear skies and minimal light pollution make it an ideal spot for watching the stars. I joined a guided stargazing tour that included a telescope and expert guidance on the constellations. It was a magical experience, and the silence of the mountains at night adds to the charm.

Stargazing Tours

Contact: Picos de Europa Adventures

Phone: +34 942 738 209

Cantabria also has a vibrant theater scene. The Palacio de Festivales de Cantabria in Santander hosts a variety of performances, including plays, dance, and concerts. The building itself is an architectural gem, and attending a show here is a wonderful way to spend an evening.

Palacio de Festivales de Cantabria

Address: Calle Gamazo, 1, 39004 Santander, Cantabria

Phone: +34 942 240 200

Finally, don't miss out on a sunset cruise along the Cantabrian coast. Several companies offer evening boat trips that provide stunning views of the coastline as the sun sets over the horizon. It's a peaceful and romantic way to end the day.

Sunset Cruises

Contact: Santander Bay Cruises

Phone: +34 942 223 362

Recap

Cantabria's nightlife has something for everyone. Whether you're in the mood for a lively bar, a night of dancing, or a relaxing evening listening to live music, you'll find it here. Exploring the nightlife gave me a deeper appreciation of Cantabria's vibrant culture and friendly locals. Each place has its own unique charm and story, making every night out an adventure. So, go out, have fun, and create some unforgettable memories in this beautiful part of Spain.

Remember to stay safe, enjoy responsibly, and immerse yourself in the local culture to truly appreciate the nightlife in Cantabria. Cheers!

Chapter 15

Shopping in Cantabria

Best Markets and Shopping Areas

Shopping in Cantabria is a delightful experience, blending the charm of traditional markets with the convenience of modern shopping areas. During my travels, I discovered some fantastic spots that cater to all tastes and budgets.

1. Mercado de la Esperanza

One of my favorite places to visit in Santander is the Mercado de la Esperanza. This bustling market is a feast for the senses, with vibrant stalls offering fresh produce, seafood, meats, and local specialties. The market is housed in a beautiful iron and glass building, a sight in itself.

Address: Plaza de la Esperanza, s/n, 39002 Santander, Cantabria

Phone: +34 942 20 30 14

I spent many mornings wandering through the aisles, chatting with vendors, and sampling delicious treats. Don't miss the chance to try some local cheeses and chorizo – they're absolutely divine.

2. Mercado del Este

For a more eclectic shopping experience, head to the Mercado del Este. This indoor market in Santander is not only a place to shop but also a cultural hub. It combines traditional market stalls with modern shops, cafes, and even an art gallery.

Address: Calle Hernán Cortés, 4, 39003 Santander, Cantabria

Phone: +34 942 21 36 08

I loved sitting at one of the cafes, sipping coffee and people-watching. The market has a great selection of local crafts and gourmet products, perfect for picking up unique souvenirs.

3. Calle Burgos

If you're looking for a mix of high street shops and local boutiques, Calle Burgos in Santander is the place to go. This lively street is lined with fashion stores, bookstores, and specialty shops. It's a great place to find both well-known brands and unique local items.

Address: Calle Burgos, 39008 Santander, Cantabria

I found some lovely handmade jewelry in a small boutique here, and it's now one of my most treasured pieces.

4. El Corte Inglés

For a more comprehensive shopping experience, El Corte Inglés is a must-visit. This department store in

Santander has everything from clothing and cosmetics to home goods and electronics. It's also a great place to find gourmet food products and local wines.

Address: Calle Alta, 19, 39008 Santander, Cantabria

Phone: +34 942 36 45 00

I spent a rainy afternoon here, exploring the different departments and picking up some gifts for friends and family.

5. Mercado de la Plaza de Abastos

In Torrelavega, the Mercado de la Plaza de Abastos is a bustling market that offers a glimpse into daily life in Cantabria. The market has a wide variety of stalls selling fresh produce, meats, fish, and local delicacies.

Address: Plaza de la Llama, s/n, 39300 Torrelavega, Cantabria

Phone: +34 942 80 13 00

I enjoyed the vibrant atmosphere and the friendly vendors, who were more than happy to share their knowledge about the local products.

What to Buy: Local Souvenirs and Products

Cantabria offers a wealth of unique souvenirs and local products that capture the essence of the region. Here are some of my favorites:

1. Quesada Pasiega

One of the most delicious souvenirs you can bring back from Cantabria is quesada pasiega, a traditional dessert made from fresh cheese, eggs, sugar, and lemon zest. It's a bit like a cheesecake but with a distinct flavor that's uniquely Cantabrian. I picked up a few slices from a bakery in Santander, and they made for a delightful treat.

2. Sobao Pasiego

Another local delicacy is sobao pasiego, a sweet, buttery cake that's perfect for breakfast or a snack. These cakes are often sold in packs, making them easy to bring home. I bought a few packs at the Mercado de la Esperanza, and they were a hit with my friends back home.

3. Cantabrian Anchovies

Cantabria is famous for its anchovies, particularly those from Santoña. These anchovies are cured and packed in olive oil, creating a rich, savory flavor. I bought a few tins from a specialty shop in Santander, and they're perfect for tapas or adding to salads.

4. Local Wines and Liqueurs

Cantabria produces some excellent wines and liqueurs. I particularly enjoyed orujo, a traditional liqueur made from grape pomace. I found a lovely bottle at El Corte

Inglés and it's a great way to bring a taste of Cantabria home with you.

5. Handcrafted Pottery

For something more permanent, consider buying some handcrafted pottery. The region has a long tradition of pottery-making, and you can find beautiful pieces at local markets and shops. I bought a charming set of ceramic mugs from a stall in the Mercado del Este, and they're now a cherished part of my kitchen.

Shopping Tips

Shopping in Cantabria is a joy, but here are a few tips to make the most of your experience:

1. Embrace the Local Markets

Local markets are a treasure trove of fresh produce, local delicacies, and unique crafts. They're also a great place to interact with locals and learn more about the region's culinary traditions. I always make it a point to visit markets early in the morning when they're at their busiest and the selection is at its best.

2. Look for Quality over Quantity

When it comes to souvenirs, I prefer quality over quantity. Handmade items, local delicacies, and unique finds make for more meaningful mementos. I found that taking the time to chat with vendors and learn about their products often led to discovering truly special items.

3. Don't Be Afraid to Haggle (Politely)

In some markets, haggling is expected and can be part of the fun. However, always do so politely and with a smile. I found that a friendly approach often led to better deals and more enjoyable interactions.

4. Bring Cash

While many shops and markets in Cantabria accept credit cards, it's always a good idea to carry some cash, especially for smaller vendors. This ensures you won't miss out on any spur-of-the-moment purchases.

5. Pack for Transport

If you're buying fragile items like pottery or bottles of wine, make sure you pack them carefully for transport. I always bring some bubble wrap and sturdy bags just in case. Most vendors are happy to help wrap your purchases securely as well.

Shopping in Cantabria is a delightful experience that goes beyond simply buying items. It's about discovering the region's culture, meeting its people, and bringing a piece of your adventure home with you. Whether you're wandering through bustling markets, exploring charming boutiques, or enjoying the convenience of department stores, each shopping trip is an opportunity to connect with Cantabria in a deeper way. So take your time, savor the experience, and happy shopping!

Chapter 16

Wellness and Relaxation

When I first arrived in Cantabria, I was immediately taken by its serene landscapes and the sense of tranquility that seemed to permeate the air. From the lush green hills to the soothing coastal breezes, this region of Spain is the perfect place to unwind and rejuvenate. If you're looking for a break from the hustle and bustle of daily life, Cantabria offers some fantastic wellness and relaxation options that you won't want to miss. Here's a comprehensive guide to the top spas, wellness centers, yoga retreats, and some personal relaxation tips based on my own experiences.

Top Spas and Wellness Centers

One of my favorite ways to relax in Cantabria is by indulging in a spa day. The region is home to several top-notch spas and wellness centers that offer a range of treatments designed to pamper and rejuvenate.

1. Balneario de Puente Viesgo

Located in the picturesque village of Puente Viesgo, this thermal spa is a haven of relaxation. The moment you step into the Balneario de Puente Viesgo, you are greeted by the soothing sounds of water and the calming scent of essential oils. The spa features natural thermal waters that are rich in minerals, perfect for soothing tired muscles and revitalizing the skin. My favorite treatment here is the hydrotherapy circuit, which includes a series of pools with varying temperatures and jets designed to massage different parts of the body.

Address: Carretera General, 78, 39670 Puente Viesgo, Cantabria

Phone: +34 942 598 061

2. Real Spa at the Hotel Real Santander

The Real Spa, located in the luxurious Hotel Real in Santander, offers a stunning view of the Bay of Santander. This spa is the epitome of elegance and tranquility. The staff is incredibly professional, and the range of treatments is extensive. I treated myself to a full-body massage followed by a facial, and it was pure bliss. The spa also features a thermal area with a heated pool, sauna, and steam room, which I highly recommend trying out.

Address: Paseo Pérez Galdós, 28, 39005 Santander, Cantabria

Phone: +34 942 272 550

3. Thalasso Real at Eurostars Hotel Real

If you're a fan of thalassotherapy, then the Thalasso Real at Eurostars Hotel Real is a must-visit. This spa uses seawater and marine products in its treatments, which are believed to have numerous health benefits. The thalassotherapy circuit here includes seawater pools, a steam bath, and a variety of marine-based treatments. I particularly enjoyed the algae wrap, which left my skin feeling incredibly soft and rejuvenated.

Address: Paseo Pérez Galdós, 28, 39005 Santander, Cantabria

Phone: +34 942 272 550

4. Templo del Agua at Castilla Termal Balneario de Solares

Nestled in the beautiful countryside of Solares, the Templo del Agua at Castilla Termal Balneario de Solares offers a unique wellness experience. The spa's "Temple of Water" features a hydrothermal circuit with therapeutic jets, a mineral-medicinal pool, and relaxation areas. The outdoor thermal pool is particularly lovely, especially on a sunny day. I spent a leisurely afternoon here, alternating between the warm thermal waters and lounging by the poolside.

Address: Calle Calvo Sotelo, 13, 39710 Solares, Cantabria

Phone: +34 942 521 313

Yoga and Meditation Retreats

For those looking to deepen their relaxation and mindfulness, Cantabria has some excellent yoga and meditation retreats. These retreats offer a peaceful environment to practice yoga, meditate, and connect with nature.

1. Yoga in Nature Retreats

One of my most memorable experiences in Cantabria was attending a Yoga in Nature retreat. Held in a charming countryside villa, these retreats combine yoga practice with outdoor activities such as hiking and beach walks. The daily yoga sessions, led by experienced instructors, were held in a serene garden setting. The retreat also included guided meditation sessions, which were perfect for quieting the mind and finding inner peace.

Address: Various locations in Cantabria (contact for details)

Phone: +34 627 935 673

2. La Casa del Yoga

Located in Santander, La Casa del Yoga is a beautiful studio offering a range of yoga classes and workshops. The instructors here are warm and welcoming, making it a great place for both beginners and experienced practitioners. I attended a weekend workshop focused on restorative yoga and mindfulness meditation, and it was a transformative experience. The studio's tranquil ambiance and the supportive community made it a truly special place to practice.

Address: Calle Floranes, 45, 39010 Santander, Cantabria

Phone: +34 646 667 428

3. Yoga North Retreats

Yoga North offers immersive yoga retreats in the stunning natural landscapes of Cantabria. These retreats typically include daily yoga sessions, meditation, and outdoor activities such as mountain hikes and coastal walks. I joined a summer retreat in the Picos de Europa mountains, and it was an unforgettable experience. Practicing yoga with a view of the majestic peaks and spending time in nature was incredibly rejuvenating.

Address: Various locations in Cantabria (contact for details)

Phone: +34 634 578 875

Relaxation Tips

After spending a considerable amount of time in Cantabria, I've gathered some personal tips on how to maximize your relaxation during your visit:

1. Embrace the Slow Pace

Cantabria is a place where life moves at a slower pace. Take the time to savor the moment, whether you're enjoying a leisurely meal at a seaside restaurant or strolling through a quaint village. Allow yourself to slow down and soak in the tranquility.

2. Connect with Nature

The natural beauty of Cantabria is one of its greatest assets. Spend time in nature, whether it's hiking in the Picos de Europa, relaxing on a secluded beach, or exploring the lush forests. Nature has a way of calming the mind and rejuvenating the spirit.

3. Indulge in Local Delicacies

Food is an integral part of the Cantabrian experience. Treat yourself to local specialties such as fresh seafood, delicious cheeses, and traditional pastries. Visit local markets and artisanal shops to discover unique flavors and products.

4. Practice Mindfulness

Incorporate mindfulness into your daily routine. Take a few moments each day to practice deep breathing, meditate, or simply sit quietly and observe your surroundings. Mindfulness helps to center yourself and enhances the overall sense of relaxation.

5. Try a New Activity

Whether it's a yoga class, a cooking workshop, or a guided nature walk, trying something new can be incredibly rewarding. It keeps your mind engaged and opens you up to new experiences and perspectives.

6. Unplug and Disconnect

Give yourself a break from the constant connectivity of modern life. Limit your screen time, turn off notifications, and be present in the moment. Use this time to read a book, write in a journal, or simply enjoy the peaceful surroundings.

7. Stay Hydrated

It's easy to forget to drink enough water, especially when you're busy exploring. Keep a water bottle with you and make sure to stay hydrated. This is particularly important if you're spending time in the sun or engaging in physical activities.

8. Get Plenty of Rest

Make sure to get a good night's sleep each night. Choose accommodation that offers a comfortable and quiet environment. If you're staying in a bustling city area, consider using earplugs or a white noise app to ensure restful sleep.

9. Pamper Yourself

Don't hesitate to indulge in some self-care. Book a massage, take a long bath, or enjoy a luxurious skincare routine. Small acts of self-care can make a big difference in how you feel.

10. Explore Mindfully

As you explore Cantabria, do so mindfully. Take the time to notice the details – the architecture, the colors, the sounds, and the smells. Being fully present enhances the experience and deepens your connection to the place.

Cantabria has a special way of making you feel at ease. Its natural beauty, rich culture, and welcoming people create an environment where relaxation comes naturally. Whether you're soaking in the thermal waters of a spa, practicing yoga in a serene garden, or simply enjoying the view of the rolling hills, Cantabria offers countless opportunities to relax and rejuvenate. I hope this guide helps you make the most of your time in this beautiful region. Enjoy your stay and take with you a renewed sense of peace and well-being.

Chapter 17

Historical Sites

Important Historical Landmarks

Cantabria is a treasure trove of historical sites that transport you back in time. Each landmark tells a story, rich with cultural and historical significance. Here are some of the most important historical landmarks that left a lasting impression on me.

1. Altamira Caves

Address: Santillana del Mar, 39330 Cantabria

Phone: +34 942 81 80 05

The Altamira Caves are often referred to as the "Sistine Chapel of Prehistoric Art," and for a good reason. When I first stepped into the replica of the caves at the Altamira Museum, I was struck by the vividness of the ancient paintings. The bison, horses, and human handprints, painted by our prehistoric ancestors around 36,000 years ago, are incredibly detailed and vibrant. The museum itself does a fantastic job of explaining the significance of these works and the lives of the people who created them.

2. Palacio de la Magdalena

Address: Avenida de la Magdalena, 1, 39005 Santander, Cantabria

Phone: +34 942 20 30 84

This majestic palace, perched on a peninsula in Santander, was originally built as a summer residence for the Spanish royal family in the early 20th century. Walking through its grand halls and elegant rooms, I could almost hear the echoes of past royalty and the laughter of high-society gatherings. The palace also offers stunning views of the Bay of Santander, making it a perfect spot for a leisurely afternoon.

3. Monastery of Santo Toribio de Liébana

Address: Calle Santo Toribio, s/n, 39570 Camaleño, Cantabria

Phone: +34 942 73 11 12

Nestled in the Picos de Europa mountains, this monastery is one of the most significant religious sites in Cantabria. It's home to the Lignum Crucis, the largest surviving piece of the True Cross. Visiting this serene and beautiful place, I felt a deep sense of peace and connection to the centuries of pilgrims who had walked these paths before me. The monastery's setting is breathtaking, surrounded by lush forests and towering peaks.

4. Cave of El Castillo

Address: Monte Castillo, s/n, 39670 Puente Viesgo, Cantabria

Phone: +34 942 59 84 25

El Castillo is another cave rich with prehistoric art, dating back over 40,000 years. The hand stencils and animal figures are mesmerizing, and the guided tour provides valuable context about the early human inhabitants of the region. As I stood inside the cool, dark cave, I marveled at the ingenuity and artistic expression of our distant ancestors.

5. Comillas and Gaudí's El Capricho

Address: Barrio Sobrellano, s/n, 39520 Comillas, Cantabria

Phone: +34 942 72 03 65

Comillas is a charming town with an impressive collection of modernist architecture, most notably El Capricho, designed by the renowned architect Antoni Gaudí. This whimsical building, adorned with sunflower tiles and intricate wrought ironwork, feels like a fairy tale come to life. Wandering through the rooms and gardens, I felt a sense of wonder and admiration for Gaudí's unique vision and creativity.

Stories Behind the Sites

Every historical site in Cantabria has its own fascinating story, adding depth and context to your visit.

1. Altamira Caves

The discovery of the Altamira Caves in 1879 by Marcelino Sanz de Sautuola and his young daughter, Maria, was initially met with skepticism. Many experts of the time couldn't believe that prehistoric people were capable of creating such sophisticated art. It wasn't until years later that the authenticity of the paintings was recognized, changing our understanding of early human history. As I explored the cave's replica, I imagined the excitement and disbelief that must have accompanied their discovery.

2. Palacio de la Magdalena

The Palacio de la Magdalena has served various purposes throughout its history. During the Spanish Civil War, it was used as a hospital and a base for the

Republican forces. Later, it became a prestigious summer school for the International University Menéndez Pelayo. Learning about these varied chapters of the palace's history added layers of meaning to my visit. I could almost see the students walking the halls, discussing ideas and enjoying the splendid views.

3. Monastery of Santo Toribio de Liébana

The Monastery of Santo Toribio de Liébana is not only a place of pilgrimage but also a center of medieval scholarship. Beatus of Liébana, a monk here, wrote his famous commentary on the Apocalypse, which was richly illustrated and widely copied throughout Europe. Standing in the monastery, I felt a profound connection to the past, imagining the monks diligently working on their manuscripts, contributing to the spread of knowledge and culture.

4. Cave of El Castillo

The Cave of El Castillo offers a unique glimpse into the lives of early humans. The paintings here are among the oldest known in the world, with some hand stencils dating back over 40,000 years. These artworks suggest a complex understanding of symbolism and communication. During my visit, the guide explained how the cave was used not only as a canvas but also as a shelter and a place of ritual. It was humbling to stand in a place where our ancestors once lived and expressed themselves.

5. Comillas and Gaudí's El Capricho

El Capricho was commissioned by Máximo Díaz de Quijano, a wealthy lawyer and music lover, who wanted a summer house that reflected his passion for music and nature. Gaudí's design includes numerous musical references, such as the piano-shaped porch and the sunflower motifs that follow the path of the sun. Walking through El Capricho, I felt a deep appreciation for the creative synergy between the client and the architect. The building is a testament to the joy of artistic collaboration and the pursuit of beauty.

Visiting Tips

Here are some tips to make the most of your visits to these historical sites in Cantabria:

1. Plan Ahead: Many of these sites, especially the caves, have limited access to preserve their delicate environments. It's a good idea to book your tickets in advance. I found that planning ahead saved me a lot of time and ensured that I didn't miss out on any must-see attractions.

2. Take Guided Tours: Guided tours are often available and provide valuable insights that you might miss on your own. The guides are usually very knowledgeable and passionate about the history of the sites. I learned so much more from the guided tours at the Altamira Caves and the Cave of El Castillo than I would have on my own.

3. Dress Comfortably: Many of these sites involve a fair amount of walking and, in the case of the caves, cool temperatures. Comfortable shoes and a light jacket are essential. I remember being glad I had layered up when I ventured into the chilly depths of El Castillo.

4. Respect the Sites: These historical landmarks are precious and need to be preserved for future generations. Follow the rules and guidelines provided, such as not touching the cave walls or staying on designated paths. Being mindful of these regulations helps protect these treasures.

5. Take Your Time: Don't rush through the sites. Take your time to soak in the history and atmosphere. Sit quietly for a few moments in the Palacio de la Magdalena's gardens or stand in awe in front of the Altamira cave paintings. These moments of reflection can be the most memorable parts of your visit.

6. Combine Visits with Local Cuisine: After a morning of exploring, I often found it rewarding to relax and

enjoy a meal at a local restaurant. For example, after visiting the Palacio de la Magdalena, I had a delightful seafood lunch at a nearby restaurant, which added to the overall experience.

Cantabria's historical sites offer a fascinating journey through time, from prehistoric cave paintings to modernist architecture. Each visit deepened my appreciation for the region's rich cultural heritage and the enduring human spirit that created these remarkable landmarks. I hope you find as much joy and inspiration in these places as I did.

Chapter 18

Festivals and Events

Visiting Cantabria was one of the most enriching experiences of my life, and the festivals and events played a significant role in that. From the vibrant streets filled with music to the intimate gatherings celebrating age-old traditions, Cantabria's festivals offer a unique glimpse into the region's soul. Here, I'll share my experiences and provide all the details you need to immerse yourself fully in Cantabria's festive spirit.

Major Annual Events

1. La Vijanera

My first encounter with Cantabria's vibrant festival culture was La Vijanera in Silió. This ancient winter masquerade, held on the first Sunday of January, is a celebration like no other. I remember being captivated by the vivid costumes, some representing animals and mythical creatures, and the elaborate face masks. The sound of cowbells filled the air as participants danced and paraded through the streets, symbolizing the expulsion of evil spirits and welcoming the New Year.

Location: Silió, Molledo

When: First Sunday of January

Contact: Ayuntamiento de Molledo, Plaza Mayor, 1, 39430 Molledo. Phone: +34 942 828 015

2. Battle of Flowers (Batalla de Flores)

Another highlight of my trip was the Battle of Flowers in Laredo. This spectacular event, held on the last Friday of August, features floats intricately decorated with thousands of vibrant flowers. The creativity and effort that go into each float are astonishing. I found a perfect spot along the parade route to admire the artistry up close. The festive atmosphere, with live music and street food, made it a delightful experience.

Location: Laredo

When: Last Friday of August

Contact: Ayuntamiento de Laredo, Plaza de la Constitución, 1, 39770 Laredo. Phone: +34 942 605 100

3. Santander International Festival (Festival Internacional de Santander)

The Santander International Festival was a cultural feast that I couldn't miss. Held every August, this month-long event brings together artists from around the world for a series of performances, including music, dance, and theater. I attended a breathtaking classical music concert at the Palacio de Festivales de Cantabria. The quality of the performances and the stunning venue left me in awe.

Location: Santander

When: August

Contact: Palacio de Festivales de Cantabria, Calle Gamazo, s/n, 39004 Santander. Phone: +34 942 240 000

4. The Virgin of Health (La Virgen de la Salud)

During my summer visit, I experienced the La Virgen de la Salud festival in Almonte. This religious celebration, held in August, includes a vibrant mix of religious processions, traditional dances, and local music. The highlight was the heartfelt procession of the Virgin's statue through the town, accompanied by prayers and songs. The sense of community and devotion was truly moving.

Location: Almonte

When: August

Contact: Ayuntamiento de Almonte, Plaza de la Constitución, 1, 21730 Almonte. Phone: +34 959 450 600

Local Celebrations and Traditions

1. Day of Cantabria (Día de Cantabria)

The Day of Cantabria in Cabezón de la Sal was an eye-opener to the region's rich cultural heritage. Celebrated on the second Sunday of August, this event showcases traditional Cantabrian music, dance, and sports. I particularly enjoyed the display of regional sports, like bolo palma (a local bowling game) and stone lifting. The town square buzzed with excitement, and I felt a part of the local community.

Location: Cabezón de la Sal

When: Second Sunday of August

Contact: Ayuntamiento de Cabezón de la Sal, Plaza del Sol, 1, 39500 Cabezón de la Sal. Phone: +34 942 700 200

2. Saint James' Day (Día de Santiago)

In Santillana del Mar, I had the chance to celebrate Saint James' Day, or Día de Santiago, on July 25th. This event, dedicated to the patron saint of Spain, includes religious ceremonies, traditional music, and a colorful market. Wandering through the medieval streets, I was captivated by the historical reenactments and the vibrant market stalls selling crafts and local delicacies.

Location: Santillana del Mar

When: July 25

Contact: Ayuntamiento de Santillana del Mar, Plaza Mayor, 1, 39330 Santillana del Mar. Phone: +34 942 818 800

3. Festival of San Roque

The Festival of San Roque in Comillas is another must-experience event. Held in mid-August, it includes a mix of religious and cultural activities. The highlight for me was the "Dance of the Arcos," where participants carry colorful arches decorated with flowers and ribbons through the town. The sense of tradition and community pride was palpable, and I loved being part of the celebrations.

Location: Comillas

When: Mid-August

Contact: Ayuntamiento de Comillas, Plaza de la Constitución, 1, 39520 Comillas. Phone: +34 942 720 115

Planning Your Visit Around Events

Planning your visit to Cantabria around these events can greatly enhance your experience. Here are some tips based on my own adventures:

1. Book Accommodation Early

Festivals in Cantabria attract many visitors, so it's wise to book your accommodation well in advance. For the Battle of Flowers in Laredo, I stayed at the Hotel Cosmopol, which offered a comfortable stay and was conveniently located near the parade route.

Hotel Cosmopol

Address: Avenida de Cantabria, 5, 39770 Laredo

Phone: +34 942 605 050

2. Arrive Early for Best Viewing Spots

Arriving early is crucial, especially for parades and major events. For La Vijanera, I reached Silió early in the morning to secure a good spot to watch the masquerade. The early start also allowed me to explore the town before it got crowded.

3. Embrace the Local Culture

Engaging with the locals can enrich your experience. During the Day of Cantabria in Cabezón de la Sal, I struck up conversations with residents who were more than happy to share the history and significance of the celebrations. Their stories added depth to my understanding of the culture.

4. Try the Festival Food

Sampling local festival food is a must. During the Santander International Festival, I enjoyed delicious regional dishes at pop-up stalls. Don't miss out on trying sobaos (a traditional sponge cake) and quesada pasiega (a cheese-based dessert).

5. Use Public Transport

Using public transport can save you the hassle of finding parking and dealing with traffic. I used the local buses and trains extensively, which were reliable and provided easy access to festival sites. The tourist information offices can provide schedules and route maps.

Tourist Information Office

Address: Plaza de Alfonso XIII, 39002 Santander

Phone: +34 942 203 000

6. Respect Local Customs

Understanding and respecting local customs can go a long way in enhancing your experience. For instance, during religious festivals like La Virgen de la Salud, dressing modestly and observing silence during processions is appreciated.

7. Extend Your Stay

If possible, extend your stay to explore more of Cantabria beyond the festival dates. After the Battle of Flowers, I spent a few extra days exploring the nearby beaches and hiking trails, which provided a perfect balance to the festive hustle and bustle.

8. Capture the Moments

Don't forget your camera or smartphone to capture the vibrant scenes. The parades, costumes, and decorations offer countless photo opportunities. Remember to respect people's privacy and ask for permission if you want to take close-up shots of participants.

Recap of Major Annual Events and Local Celebrations

La Vijanera

Location: Silió, Molledo

When: First Sunday of January

Contact: Ayuntamiento de Molledo, Plaza Mayor, 1, 39430 Molledo. Phone: +34 942 828 015

Battle of Flowers

Location: Laredo

When: Last Friday of August

Contact: Ayuntamiento de Laredo, Plaza de la Constitución, 1, 39770 Laredo. Phone: +34 942 605 100

Santander International Festival

Location: Santander

When: August

Contact: Palacio de Festivales de Cantabria, Calle Gamazo, s/n, 39004 Santander. Phone: +34 942 240 000

The Virgin of Health

Location: Almonte

When: August

Contact: Ayuntamiento de Almonte, Plaza de la Constitución, 1, 21730 Almonte. Phone: +34 959 450 600

Day of Cantabria

Location: Cabezón de la Sal

When: Second Sunday of August

Contact: Ayuntamiento de Cabezón de la Sal, Plaza del Sol, 1, 39500 Cabezón de la Sal. Phone: +34 942 700 200

Saint James' Day

Location: Santillana del Mar

When: July 25

Contact: Ayuntamiento de Santillana del Mar, Plaza Mayor, 1, 39330 Santillana del Mar. Phone: +34 942 818 800

Festival of San Roque

Location: Comillas

When: Mid-August

Contact: Ayuntamiento de Comillas, Plaza de la Constitución, 1, 39520 Comillas. Phone: +34 942 720 115

Appendix

Enhance Your Cantabria Experience

Cantabria is a region that captivates with its diverse landscapes, rich history, and vibrant culture. Here are some tips and resources to help you make the most of your visit.

Map of Cantabria

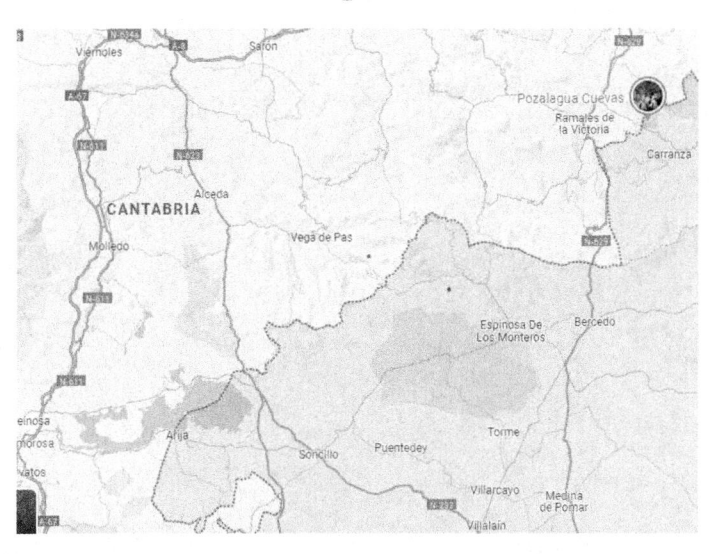

https://maps.app.goo.gl/zuJ7RuYeKtZ4gQ4W9

SCAN THE
IMAGE/QR CODE
WITH YOUR
PHONE TO GET
THE LOCATIONS
IN REAL TIME.

Map of Things to do in Cantabria

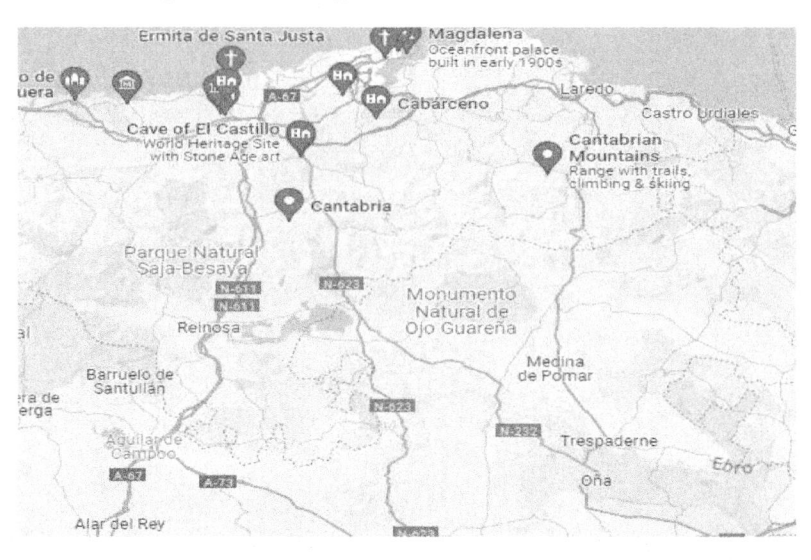

https://www.google.com/maps/search/things+to+do+in+Cantabria++/@43.1349804,-4.6601485,9z/data=!3m1!4b1?entry=ttu

SCAN THE IMAGE/QR CODE WITH YOUR PHONE TO GET THE LOCATIONS IN REAL TIME.

Glossary: Local Terms

Understanding a few local terms can enhance your experience in Cantabria. Here are some that I found particularly useful:

Barrio: Neighborhood

Plaza: Square

Pincho: A small snack typically eaten in bars

Sidra: Cider, a popular local drink

Montaña: Mountain, often used to refer to the inland regions

Applications and Useful Resources

Technology can greatly enhance your travel experience. Here are some apps and resources that I found incredibly helpful:

Google Maps: For navigation and finding local attractions, restaurants, and shops.

TripAdvisor: For reviews and recommendations on places to visit and eat.

Google Translate: Useful for translating menus and signs if your Spanish is a bit rusty.

Cantabria Turística: The official tourism app provides comprehensive information on events, attractions, and more.

XE Currency Converter: Handy for converting prices if you're coming from outside the Eurozone.

Addresses and Locations of Popular Accommodations

Cantabria offers a range of accommodations to suit all budgets. Here are some popular ones:

1. Hotel Altamira

Address: Calle Canton, 1, 39330 Santillana del Mar, Cantabria

Phone: +34 942 81 80 01

2. Abba Comillas Golf Hotel

Address: Urbanización Rovacías, s/n, 39520 Comillas, Cantabria

Phone: +34 942 72 14 50

3. Gran Hotel Sardinero

Address: Plaza de Italia, 1, 39005 Santander, Cantabria

Phone: +34 942 27 10 00

4. Hotel Valdecoro

Address: Avenida de España, 20, 39570 Potes, Cantabria

Phone: +34 942 73 80 25

5. Hostal Jardin Secreto

Address: Calle del Cardenal Cisneros, 37, 39007 Santander, Cantabria

Phone: +34 942 37 59 01

Addresses and Locations of Popular Restaurants and Cafes

Cantabria's culinary scene is vibrant and diverse. Here are some of my favorite restaurants and cafes:

1. Casa Cossío

Address: Plaza Mayor, 12, 39330 Santillana del Mar, Cantabria

Phone: +34 942 81 81 15

2. Restaurante El Remedio

Address: Carretera de la Playa de Luaña, s/n, 39527 Ruiloba, Cantabria

Phone: +34 942 72 61 25

3. El Pescador

Address: Calle Padre Antonio, 4, 39540 San Vicente de la Barquera, Cantabria

Phone: +34 942 71 52 40

4. Bodega del Riojano

Address: Calle del Rio de la Pila, 5, 39003 Santander, Cantabria

Phone: +34 942 21 45 82

5. Restaurante Casa Cayo

Address: Calle San Roque, 3, 39570 Potes, Cantabria

Phone: +34 942 73 80 06

Addresses and Locations of Top Attractions

Make sure to visit these top attractions during your stay in Cantabria:

1. Altamira Caves

Address: Santillana del Mar, 39330 Cantabria

Phone: +34 942 81 80 05

2. Palacio de la Magdalena

Address: Avenida de la Magdalena, 1, 39005 Santander, Cantabria

Phone: +34 942 20 30 84

3. Monastery of Santo Toribio de Liébana

Address: Calle Santo Toribio, s/n, 39570 Camaleño, Cantabria

Phone: +34 942 73 11 12

4. Cave of El Castillo

Address: Monte Castillo, s/n, 39670 Puente Viesgo, Cantabria

Phone: +34 942 59 84 25

5. Comillas and Gaudí's El Capricho

Address: Barrio Sobrellano, s/n, 39520 Comillas, Cantabria

Phone: +34 942 72 03 65

Photo Attribution

https://www.freepik.com/free-photo/view-murcia-bridge-segura_1584031.htm#fromView=search&page=1&position=8&uuid=3a2dd839-d57f-4b2f-979f-ca13b20d8e58

https://maps.app.goo.gl/Tygun3NHiwba9vxW6

https://www.freepik.com/free-photo/plaza-de-espana-monument-with-fountain-barcelona-spain-cloudy-sky-traffic_16449564.htm#fromView=search&page=2&position=26&uuid=c40f43f9-be7a-4c5f-8606-e530adeab86c

https://www.freepik.com/free-photo/beautiful-tropical-beach-sea-with-coconut-palm-tree-paradise-island_3661769.htm#fromView=search&page=9&position=42&uuid=d6136939-942b-4463-a067-7832bedf74dc

https://www.freepik.com/free-photo/view-prague-by-night_10585715.htm#fromView=search&page=1&position=23&uuid=10b48138-a4b8-4236-bb86-3f7d92479869

SCAN TO SEE ALL BOOKS ABOUT DIFFERENT CITIES AND ISLANDS IN SPAIN.

Printed in Great Britain
by Amazon